Fiesta

for the

Hispanic

Soul

Fiesta

for the

Hispanic

Soul

Over 60 stories and poems to inspire and motivate you

Stories and poems by Ruben Soto

iUniverse, Inc.
New York Lincoln Shanghai

Fiesta for the Hispanic Soul

iUniverse, Inc.

For information address:
iUniverse, Inc.
2021 Pine Lake Road, Suite 100
Lincoln, NE 68512
www.iuniverse.com

ISBN: 0-595-29940-7

Printed in the United States of America

In memory of my father and mother.
I will always love you both.

Contents

4. OUR FAMILY

5. GRIEF AND DISAPPOINTMENTS

6. RICH, FAMOUS, AND HISPANIC

7. LOVE

8. OUR FOODS

9. PERSONAL TREASURES

Introduction

It was not my intention to write an inspirational book for Hispanics as my first book. But my disillusionment with the lack of literature, for and about Hispanics, compelled me to do it. I just couldn't believe that Latinos were being ignored and alienated by the literary world.

As a writer, I like to read a lot, so I visit bookstores frequently. I always make it a point to visit the Hispanic section, to see what's new. And, to my disappointment, there usually is nothing new. Most of the contemporary books written by Hispanic authors are non-appealing, to an educated middle-class Hispanic, like myself. Many of my successful Hispanic friends share the same sentiment. We are all frustrated at the manner in which the mainstream media still likes to portray us. The books we find about Hispanics are either about people in the barrio, gang members, someone in prison, or people who are just plain poor.

What about the rest of us? What about those of us who have made something of ourselves, and live ordinary American lives, and want the best for our family, and for those close to us? What about those of us who are college-educated, and have achieved the coveted middle-class status, and who enjoy the finer things in life? What about those of us who have successfully assimilated into the American culture, but yet are proud of our Hispanic heritage? There is hardly anything out there for us to read.

I was determined to change that. I wanted to write a book that inspired and motivated all Hispanics—those here in America and those who dream of coming here someday. America is the land of opportunity, and the land where dreams do come true. It is a shame that we Latinos have one of the highest levels of high school dropouts. And unfortunately, one of the lowest percentages of college graduates. We have to change that. One way of doing this is by changing the negative stereotype that has been given to us. By writing books that create a different and more positive image of us is a good start. This may get our young people to start reading success stories, and start believing in themselves. Then, it will create a domino effect—more books will be written, the media will take notice, and so will the major companies, causing attitudes to change. It will create more successful and educated Hispanics. We have to show the nation that we are not an uneducated group; we just simply have been brushed aside.

Latinos are very diverse, and it is very hard to categorize us under one umbrella. But what we have in common is the love for our traditions, our foods, our extended families, and our heritage. We are now living in the greatest country in the world, which offers us the opportunity to achieve success at all levels. We have already made a difference. Just look all around you and you will see the Hispanic influence in American life. *Que rico!*

I thoroughly enjoyed taking the time to write these stories and poems, because I wanted to make a difference. I am proud of my Hispanic heritage, and my culture merits to have the same respect that other cultures have attained.

Fiesta for the Hispanic Soul is a book whose time is well overdue. My goal is to keep writing more of these stories, and share them with you and the rest of the world. We have a unique culture, and only a Hispanic writer is able to interpret and write about it.

I owe my parents a great deal of thanks, for sacrificing their lives by coming to America. Like many other Cubans, who fled Cuba in the 1960's, they left everything behind, not knowing what the future had in store for them. But they had a strong faith in God, and that's what kept their dreams alive. More than anything, they sacrificed their lives for us, their children, so that we could have a better life. They are both gone now from this earth, but they still live inside of me—deep within my thoughts.

I had the privilege of growing up in a predominantly Mexican-American culture, and I came to embrace it as my own. I thank God that he gave me the opportunity to become a part of that culture too. I truly understand both cultures very well. But most important, I am thankful that I have also embraced the American culture. I have many Anglo friends, who have motivated me and who have served as role models and inspiration for me. So, I have the best of three cultures. I couldn't have asked for anything better.

Hispanics enjoy fiestas because they always like to be happy. Most of the stories will inspire you, some will make you think, others may make you cry, and some will propel you to succeed. I hope you share them with your friends, and I hope they will make you happy to be alive, to be Hispanic or Latino, and to be an American.

So sit back, relax, and enjoy reading the stories and poems about our people and our culture.

Let the fiesta begin!

EVERYTHING IS
POSSIBLE IN AMERICA

Hispanic

Am I Hispanic?
I often ask myself this question.
What is this label that I've been given?
Hispanic can mean a lot of things.
To those of us who grew up in Hispanic families
it means that we are of a special culture.
But to others who don't understand us
it means we are a category between white and black.
How sad that we aren't given the chance to
explain who we really are.
We are composed of various ethnic groups
forced to be categorized under one label.
Hispanics, or Latinos, are of different nationalities:
Spaniard, Mexican, Cuban, Puerto Rican, Colombian, Venezuelan,
Argentinean, Dominican, Peruvian, Panamanian, Nicaraguan,
Costa Rican, Honduran, Salvadoran, Guatemalan, Bolivian,
Chilean, Uruguayan, Paraguayan, Brazilian, Ecuadorian,
All of us have different foods, traditions and customs that
help us identify with our roots.
Contrary to the misconception, not all Hispanics eat the same foods.
We eat paella, flour and corn tortillas, black beans and rice, pigeon peas and rice,
plantains, grilled steaks, pork roast, tamales of different flavors and ingredients.
Not all Hispanics eat spicy foods either, it depends on the country
that our ancestors were from. Traditional Spaniard and Cuban foods are rich
in spices that add to the flavor, but they're not hot.
Traditional Mexican food is both spicy and hot and delicious.
For those of us that have had the privilege of being raised in
different Hispanic cultures, we can appreciate all of these traditions and foods.
I love being Hispanic, I love being an American.
America has brought us all together and we must learn from each other.
We must be content being categorized under one label.

There are many more similarities that unite us as one.
Let's not let our differences keep us divided.
How thankful I am that I have been exposed to many different cultures.
For I have learned to appreciate life by being introduced to many people.
Don't despise another culture because it's different than yours.
Let's let our different cultures and traditions bring us together.
The next time you meet a person from another Hispanic culture,
ask them if you can learn more about their culture, foods, and traditions.
It will be one of the most thrilling experiences in your life.
This has certainly worked for me, and I know it will do the same for you too.
I am Hispanic and proud!

Only In America Do Dreams Come True

Only in America can a young and determined Cuban man ever dream of becoming a TV legend. The late Desi Arnaz achieved this dream.

Only in America can a poor but determined Mexican-American have ever dreamed of making a difference for many Hispanic generations to come. The late Cesar Chavez achieved this dream.

Only in America can a young man from Chile ever dream of becoming Spanish television's most recognizable entertainer. Just ask Mario Kreutzberger, otherwise known as Don Francisco of Univision's *Sabado Gigante* fame.

Only in America could a Cuban immigrant become the President of the Coca-Cola Company. The late Roberto Goizueta achieved this dream.

Only in America can a poor Mexican-American girl ever dream of marrying into a dynasty, and becoming the first lady of Florida. Just ask Columba Bush, wife of Jeb Bush, Governor of Florida (son of former President George Bush and brother of current President George W. Bush).

Only in America can a Spaniard man born with a talented voice ever dream of becoming one of opera's greatest singers. Just ask Placido Domingo.

Only in America can a Cuban-American woman become the most successful and famous crossover singer of all times. Only in America could her husband become one of music's greatest producers. Just ask Gloria and Emilio Estefan.

Only in America can a poor Mexican-American boy grow up to be the mayor of a large city, the head of the national HUD program and the president of Univision. Just ask Henry Cisneros.

Only in America can a poor Mexican-American girl hope to make her dreams of becoming an international singer come true. Just ask Vicki Carr.

Only in America can a poor Mexican immigrant man dream of becoming a national television anchor. Just ask Univision anchor Jorge Ramos.

Only in America can a beautiful and talented Cuban-American girl aspire to become Univision's first female news anchor. Just ask Teresa Rodriguez.

Only in America can a poor Mexican-American girl from Los Angeles grow up to be the anchor for a national television newscast. Just ask Univision anchor Maria Elena Salinas.

Only in America can a beautiful Puerto Rican girl aspire to become a TV personality in both Spanish and English. Just ask Telemundo/NBC's Maria Celeste Arraras.

Only in America can a young Cuban-American man dream of having a successful lifelong career on Spanish television. Just ask Jesse Losada of Telemundo.

Only in America can a poor but intelligent young Mexican-American man dream of becoming a national television correspondent. Just ask John Quiñones of ABC TV.

Only in America can a young Cuban-American woman make her dream come true of becoming a national anchor. Just ask Soledad O'Brien of CNN and formerly of NBC's *Today Show*.

Only in America can a young Cuban-American girl from Miami dream of becoming the first Hispanic woman to host NBC's *Today Show*. Just ask Jackie Nespral.

Only in America can a young Cuban-American man dream of ever having success as a TV personality in both the English and Spanish markets. Just ask Jose Diaz-Balart formerly of CBS and now with Telemundo.

Only in America can a talented young Mexican-American man ever dream of one day anchoring the national news on CNN. Just ask Renay San Miguel.

Only in America can a Puerto Rican/Jewish man aspire to become famous for his unique television reporting. Just ask Geraldo Rivera.

Only in America can a talented young boy from the Dominican Republic ever dream of becoming one of baseball's highest paid players. Just ask Alex Rodriguez.

Only in America can a poor but driven boy from the Dominican Republic ever have become a baseball legend in his living years. Just ask Sammy Sosa.

Only in America can a young Cuban-American man ever dream of becoming a major league baseball player and setting a home run record. Just ask Rafael Palmeiro.

Only in America can a poor Mexican-American boy from East Los Angeles ever dream of winning an Olympic Gold Medal and then become a successful boxer. Just ask Oscar de la Hoya.

Only in America can a poor Mexican-American boy ever dream of becoming a golf legend. Just ask Lee Trevino.

Only in America can a blonde Cuban-American bombshell ever dream of becoming a respected Hollywood actress and sex symbol at the same time. Just ask Cameron Diaz.

Only in America can a handsome and talented Puerto Rican man become a well-known Hollywood actor. Just ask Jimmy Smits.

Only in America can a Cuban-American become the nation's most famous home repair guru. Just ask Bob Vila.

Only in America can a Puerto Rican girl from New York dream of becoming the highest paid Hispanic actress in Hollywood. Just ask Jennifer Lopez.

Only in America can a Puerto Rican woman dream of winning an Oscar, a Tony, and an Emmy. Just ask Rita Moreno.

Only in America can a middle-aged Cuban woman have phenomenal success with her own national Spanish television talk show. Just ask Cristina Saralegui.

Only in America can a former Mexican soap opera star believe she can succeed in Hollywood, even with her limited English fluency. Add to that, being nominated for an Oscar in such little time. Just ask Salma Hayek.

Only in America can a poor Mexican-American boy from California become one of the world's premier musicians for almost five decades. Just ask Carlos Santana.

Only in America can a young, beautiful, and talented Mexican-American singer ever dream of becoming a pop music icon. Just ask Linda Rondstadt.

Only in America can a young Puerto Rican girl dream of becoming the nation's Surgeon General. Just ask Antonia Novello.

Only in America can a Mexican immigrant ever dream of becoming the nation's treasurer. Just ask former U.S. Treasurer Rosario Marin.

Only in America can a talented Mexican actor aspire to be a leading Hollywood actor. The late Anthony Quinn achieved this dream.

Only in America can a young Mexican-American man ever fulfill his dream of becoming a serious actor in Hollywood. Just ask Edward James Olmos.

Only in America can a young Cuban-American actor aspire to become a leading Hollywood actor. Just ask Andy Garcia.

Only in America can a distinguished and determined young Mexican actor become one of Hollywood's most recognized actors. Just ask Ricardo Montalban.

Only in America can a handsome and talented Spanish actor become one of Hollywood's sexiest men. Just ask Antonio Banderas.

Only in America can a poor Mexican-American comedian dream of becoming a national and world celebrity. Just ask either Paul Rodriguez or George Lopez.

Only in America can a beautiful, young Hispanic woman become the symbol of American beauty. Just ask former Miss USA and actress Laura Herring, and Susie Castillo, Miss USA 2003.

Only in America can a beautiful and talented Cuban-American girl ever dream of becoming a TV personality. Just ask Daisy Fuentes.

Only in America can a multi-talented young Mexican-American girl have success in the contemporary Christian music world, and at the same time attain greater success in the Latin music segment. Just ask Jaci Velasquez.

Only in America can an exotic looking Hispanic girl dream of becoming one of Hollywood's most recognized sex symbols. Just ask Raquel Welch.

Only in America can a young Puerto Rican man dream of becoming a respected actor. The late Raul Julia achieved it.

Only in America can a person of Hispanic descent dream of becoming the governor of one of the states. Ask former Florida governor Bob Martinez and New Mexico's governor Bill Richardson.

Only in America can a young Cuban-American woman dream of one day being an integral part of the U.S. Congress. Just ask Ileana Ros-Lehtinen of Florida, the first Hispanic woman elected in Congress.

Only in America can an intelligent Cuban-American man ever dream that one day he would represent his state in the national congress. Just ask Robert Menendez of New Jersey.

Only in America can a Mexican-American ever dream of becoming one of the wealthiest men in the country and becoming the first Hispanic to run for Governor of Texas. Just ask Tony Sanchez.

Only in America can any Hispanic become a member of Congress. The following are either past or present members of our nation's Congress:
Anibal Acevedo-Vila, Joe Baca, Herman Badillo, Xavier Becerra, Henry Bonilla, Dennis Cardoza, Eligio "Kika" de la Garza II, Lincoln Diaz-Balart, Mario Diaz-Balart, Robert Garcia, Charles A. Gonzalez, Henry B. Gonzalez, Raul M. Grijalva, Luis V. Gutierrez, Ruben Hinojosa, Manuel Lujan, Matthew Martinez, Grace Napolitano, Dennis Nunes, Solomon Ortiz, Ed Lopez Pastor, Silvestre Reyes, Ciro Rodriguez, Edward Roybal-Allard, Lucille Roybal-Allard, Linda Sanchez, Loretta Sanchez, Jose Serrano, Hilda L. Solis, Frank Tejeda, Esteban Torres, and Nydia Velasquez.

Only in America can a young and intelligent Mexican-American man ever dream of becoming the mayor of one of the nation's largest cities. Just ask San Antonio's mayor Ed Garza.

Only in America can five Hispanic men ever dream of becoming mayor of Miami, the most Hispanic city in the nation. Just ask Mauricio Ferre, Xavier Suarez, Joe Carollo, Manny Diaz and Alex Penelas (Miami-Dade mayor).

Only in America can a talented black Cuban woman dream of becoming the world's ambassador for salsa music. The late Celia Cruz achieved this dream.

Only in America can a poor and talented Mexican-American girl dream of becoming the queen of Tejano music, and being loved by many around the world. The late Selena achieved this dream.

Only in America can a talented young Puerto Rican man dream of becoming the King of Salsa. The late Tito Puente achieved this dream.

Only in America can a little girl make her dreams come true by first being a Mousketeer, and then a pop music sensation. Just ask Cristina Aguilera.

Only in America can a handsome, young Puerto Rican boy dream of becoming one of music's greatest stars. Just ask Ricky Martin.

Only in America can a Spanish singer with limited English skills dream of becoming a successful entertainer. Just ask Julio Iglesias.

Only in America can the son of a popular Spanish singer dream of having more success than his father. Just ask Enrique Iglesias.

Only in America can a poor Puerto Rican boy from New York ever dream of becoming a famous international singer in both English and Spanish. Just ask Marc Anthony.

Only in America can Latin singers dream of having crossover success into the American music scene. Just ask Shakira, Thalia, and Juanes.

Only in America can eight intelligent and determined Hispanics ever dream of becoming astronauts in the NASA Space Program. Just ask Franklin Chang-Diaz, Michael Lopez-Alegria, Fernando Caldeiro, Carlos Noriega, Christopher Loria, George Zamka, Danny Olivas and Ellen Ochoa (the only Hispanic woman astronaut).

Only in America!

Ana

She grabbed her suitcase and took one last look at her room.
This had been her home for many years.
The memories would stay with her forever.
She remembers how poor her family was.
How sometimes there was hardly any food on the table.
But somehow her parents had the strength to work hard.
They wanted their children to become professionals.
She was the middle child and the smartest one.
Today she was moving from her home in East Los Angeles.
She was headed to Princeton to study History.
Then she would continue to Law School.
She was the first one in her family to attend college.
She had been awarded a scholarship for her outstanding grades.
She would be flying for the first time in her life.
She knew that once she left this place, she would never be the same.
She hugged and kissed her mother first, then her father.
She said goodbye to her brothers and sisters.
And she was off to the airport.
Her new life was just beginning.

It's Your Choice

Many before us have come to America seeking a better life.

Many have succeeded.

Many have failed.

Those who succeeded worked hard to get there.

Those who failed simply sat back and got complacent.

America offers you many opportunities to succeed.

You just have to give success a try.

Many will come after us who are hungry for success.

Why let them take our piece of the pie away from us?

You will either succeed.

Or you will fail.

It's up to you.

It's your choice.

I Want To Be A Boxer

The little boy walked into the old, smelly gym, and saw his brother from a distance. His brother was practicing with another boy; they were throwing punches at each other. An older man was standing in the ring with them, guiding their every move.

As the little boy approached the ring, he saw other boys watching intensely, as the two boxers fought with each other. Suddenly, the little boy felt a strange sensation flowing through his body. He was excited at the sight of the two boys boxing. He envisioned himself becoming a boxer too.

He saw two gloves lying on a chair, and he took them in his hands. He put them on and started throwing punches. He imagined he was a professional boxer and he was invincible. The old man saw him, and asked him if he wanted to join the boxing league. The eager little boy didn't have to think twice about it.

He was now a boxer, and it was up to him to determine what the outcome would be. Will he become a professional boxer and turn his life around? Or would he lose hope and live in the slums forever? Only he will be able to make this decision.

Our Awards and Our Magazines

I remember, only fifteen years ago, how embarrassing it was for many of us to hear someone singing in Spanish on national English television. Those of us who grew up in bilingual homes wanted to hide any time this happened. We didn't want to be associated with the singer or their song. How silly, since we didn't seem to mind if we were watching it on Spanish television. But it was taboo on an English station. This negative thinking was the result of what we were taught in school—speaking Spanish was wrong. It was almost synonymous to committing a sin, or an immoral act.

Shortly after my family arrived in the United States, in the late 1960's, we moved to a small Texas town. My father was a minister, and he was assigned to pastor a local Spanish-speaking church. It was the time in our country where segregation still existed. The town was divided by the railroad tracks—the Anglos lived on one side and the Hispanics on the other.

I remember getting a spanking from my Anglo second-grade teacher, because some kid told her that I had said a bad word in Spanish. It wasn't a bad word at all—it was just *Cuban Spanish*, which he didn't understand. My mother noticed how the paddle had left its mark on my behind, while changing my clothes when I got home.

The following day my father put on his best suit, and had a conference with the teacher. No son of his was going to be treated in that manner. How I appreciate his courage now that I look back on this incident. He knew that there had been a misunderstanding, and he wanted to clarify the situation. He explained our status as recent immigrants, and his job as a pastor.

I became the teacher's pet after my father's talk with her, and my grades improved dramatically. The following year I was placed in a class for advanced students.

I bring up this story since many of us have a negative perception of speaking Spanish. Many Hispanic parents throughout the generations have deprived their children of the beauty of knowing Spanish. They wanted their children to be proficient in English, so they wouldn't suffer the kind of discrimination that they were used to. But how times have changed. Now it's trendy and necessary to know both languages well.

I remember as a kid, watching *The Lawrence Welk Show* with my mother, who absolutely loved it. It helped introduce us to the American way of life, in a sense. I recall watching the Hispanic singer, Ana Cani, singing in Spanish with no shame whatsoever, and getting ovations from the predominant Anglo audience.

Years later, Gloria Estefan shocked many when she sang in Spanish on a national music awards show. I was living in Miami at the time and the next day at work I heard a Cuban-American woman say, "Why did Gloria have to sing in Spanish? It was so embarrassing!" More power to you Gloria since you were proud of your heritage and you were showing the rest of the country what was yet to come.

It was Gloria and Emilio Estefan's dream to start the Latin Grammys and I remember the controversy that brewed with the first show. However, what I remember the most was how well coordinated it turned out to be. Many Americans were introduced to our Spanish lyrics and rhythms for the first time in their life. And they were also introduced to a new Colombian singer named Shakira, who dazzled the audience that evening.

I just finished watching the latest edition of the Latin Grammys, where another Colombian singer named Juanes swept the awards. It started with a terrific tribute to the late Celia Cruz, who we just recently lost. The featured entertainers all sang in Spanish, although the entire show was in English. This is America today. It is no longer embarrassing to hear Spanish on English TV. Today we are proud of the accomplishments we have made, and are starting to be accepted in the mainstream media.

I watched the recent Hispanic Heritage Awards, and it was great to see so many accomplished Hispanics in different fields. The first award went to Sonia Manzano, who is best known as Maria from *Sesame Street*. With pride, she accepted the award, and told the audience how honored she feels having represented Latinos in that all-time popular show. She relayed how she grew up in the South Bronx, and there were no Latino role models on TV.

The other recipients included Linda Chavez-Thompson, a labor movement leader; Denise Chavez for literature; and Omar Minaya, of the Montreal Expos, who is the first Hispanic manager of a baseball team.

It was a great and inspirational show, that more than likely, motivated many to pursue their dreams.

The other great accomplishment has been our recent surge of magazines dedicated to Hispanics. Perhaps the one with the greatest tenure and the best known is *Hispanic.* This magazine has dedicated itself to profile successful Hispanics in all areas of life. I am sure it has not been easy trying to please all of the different Latinos in our country. But its formula seems to be working, and it keeps uniting us all.

Hispanic Business has been the other successful magazine. It is another source for inspiration and motivation, since it features many Hispanic entrepreneurs, and those moving up the corporate ladder, or already there.

The great thing about both of these magazines is that they have their own web sites, and updated information is readily available.

How good it really feels that we have accomplished all of these significant goals, to improve the image of all Hispanics in America.

SUCCESS

The Hispanic Success Guru:
Lionel Sosa

The event was to be held in a San Antonio Hispanic Chamber of Commerce breakfast. He would be the speaker that morning, and he was going to talk about his new book *The Americano Dream: How Latinos Can Achieve Success in Business and in Life.* I convinced a young co-worker to go with me, since he was a young up-and-coming Hispanic manager. I saw the drive in him, and I wanted him to focus on succeeding and not giving up. He had just graduated with a business degree, and I wanted him to get motivated about moving up the corporate ladder. What better way to get motivated than to attend this breakfast featuring Lionel Sosa?

This was in the spring of 1998, and I didn't want to be stuck in a customer service supervisor job all of my life. I wanted to become someone that made a difference in this world. I was proficient in both English and Spanish, and I wanted a job where I could use these skills more thoroughly. My Anglo managers didn't appreciate or understand my drive and special skills. They didn't see beyond my ethnicity, and I wasn't given the opportunity to advance to a higher management position. I learned the hard way the impact that politics has on one's business success. *"It's not what you know, but who you know, that will get you to where you want to be"*, as the old adage says. I wanted out of the corporate world, and I wanted to have my own business. But first I needed to have someone motivate me, and I knew by coming to hear Mr. Sosa would be a great start.

I loved his speech that morning, inspiring and motivating the mostly Hispanic crowd of professionals to believe in their dream. I remember talking to those that were in my table. I remember specifically one distinguished lady who was there with her son. She was excited because her son was planning on starting a business using a web page. She was describing with excitement this new technology. Back then I still didn't have a personal computer, so I wasn't quite familiar with how this worked. I recall laughing secretly at her description of this new technology, and thinking if it wasn't just another scam. Little did I know how big this would become.

After his speech, Mr. Sosa accepted questions from the crowd, and then towards the latter part he took time to sign copies of his book. My co-worker and I purchased copies, which were already autographed, but we wanted to meet him in person. I remember when it was my turn I told him what an inspiration he was. He dedicated the book to me, and I went home and read the entire book in about a week. I would quote many of the book's advice to any young Hispanic that I met who wanted to have professional success. One of these was a new supervisor, who after reading the book became more apt to succeed, and became a huge fan of Mr. Sosa.

Eventually I left my corporate job to start a gourmet coffee business. Although the business failed, it gave me a new outlook in life and opened new opportunities. I met many new people and I was introduced to poetry readings and to several writers. It introduced me to a whole new world. It introduced me to a whole new me. It gave birth to a writer.

Thank you, Lionel Sosa, for instilling this sense of achievement in me.

A Young Man's Success Story

The tired old man could not believe his eyes. He could never have imagined owning such a beautiful car. But there it was in front of him—a shiny new Jaguar. This was a gift from his son, who was grateful for having had such a loving father.

This father had come to America from Cuba many years ago. He had lost everything there, and now he had to make a new life in this new country. All he could think of then was how he was going to provide for his family. But he was used to hard work, and immediately found work in a factory. He never learned English well, so for the rest of his life he only worked at factories. His wife dedicated herself to cleaning houses, and added to the family's income.

Both of them had a strong faith in God, and they raised their son and daughter in a positive environment. The children were very active in their local church, and they also excelled in school. But it was their son who would have the greatest success. After graduating from high school with honors, he received a scholarship to attend the University of Florida. He graduated with a History degree in the top five percent of his class. He was now ready for law school, and was awarded a scholarship from three different law schools: University of Miami, University of Texas, and Harvard.

The choice was his to make, and he thought it would be simple. "Hey, if I choose the University of Miami, I can study and party at the same time. The beach will be only a few minutes away. If I choose the University of Texas, I can study and party on Sixth Street. And if I choose Harvard, well, what is there to do up there anyway?" he said.

An attorney, from a law firm who was interested in hiring him after graduation from law school, invited him to have lunch one day. He listened to the young man's reasoning and then offered him his advice. He told him the only intelligent choice was obviously Harvard. For it had the most respected law school in the nation, and it was an honor for him to be offered a scholarship at this prestigious school. Not only that, but having a law degree from Harvard would open doors everywhere. And he would be compensated very well, something that the other schools could not guarantee.

The young man took his advice and went to Harvard. He eventually graduated with honors and was offered a position in that law firm. As the years went
by, this young man became a distinguished lawyer, and now he is the Chief Legal
Counsel for one of the most powerful companies in the nation.

Now, a man of status, this former aspiring lawyer attributes his success to his
father's sacrifice and his mother's love. But most important of all, he is thankful
to God for the wonderful parents he gave him. He is now married to a very beautiful lady, and he is a proud father himself.

He was moved with emotion seeing how touched his father felt by his generous gift. He will never know all of the sacrifice his parents went through to come
to this country. He has only heard the stories. This is only one way that he could
repay back the love they bestowed on him.

Successful Hispanic Women

It has never been tradition for Hispanic women to aspire to become professionals after high school. However, we have seen a change in this area within the last twenty years. A Hispanic woman's role was always that of a housewife and a mother. But never was she supposed to go out on her own and make a career for herself. But, how times have changed.

Three successful Hispanic women come to mind. All three came from traditional Hispanic homes, where there was both a father and a mother. All of these women were raised with good moral values, and their parents encouraged them to pursue professional careers. They knew that this was the only way their daughters could be successful in this country.

One of these women became a pharmacist. She remembers how nervous her parents were when she drove five hundred miles to attend college. Her father stood by the phone whenever she would travel back and forth. This was completely unheard of in their generation. A woman was not supposed to venture on her own like that. But they had to accept the fact that times had changed and they were in a new country. After her college experience they were surprised as to how "Americanized" their daughter had become. She found a great paying job after graduating as a pharmacist, and she helped raise her family's standard of living.

Another Hispanic woman studied to become a chiropractor. She was a third generation Hispanic, since her parents were born in America. They had no problem with their daughter going away to college. They were very proud of her when she opened her own practice. She has become an inspiration to other Hispanic women.

The last woman studied to become an accountant. She also went away to college, and she was the first one in her family to do this. Her mother finally approved of her moving away to attend college, after much convincing from her daughter. The mother called her everyday to make sure she was all right. This young woman eventually became a partner at the accounting firm where she has worked for over five years. She is the only Hispanic partner in the firm. She just purchased an expensive import car, and bought land in an exclusive area, where she will eventually build her elaborate home.

A Tale of Two Men:
Robert and Joe

This is the story of two Hispanic guys who grew up in California, Robert Martinez and Joe Gutierrez.

Robert was a bright kid, and his parents knew that their son was special. His parents had moved to Los Angeles many years ago from Tijuana, Mexico. They wanted a better life for their children, and America was the only country where they could make this happen. Besides Robert, they had five other children, three boys and two girls. Robert was the middle child.

Robert's father was a carpenter, and he worked at low paying jobs for many years. His mother was a seamstress, and she worked hard to give the best to her children. They soon realized that life in America was not easy. But nevertheless they continued to work hard knowing that it would pay off eventually. The reward would be seeing their children successful someday.

Robert always got A's in his report card, and was without a doubt, the smartest one in the family. He graduated with honors from high school, making his parents very proud. He received a full scholarship to Stanford University, and then went on to medical school. He is now a successful surgeon, and has a lovely wife, and two children.

When asked what drove him to succeed, when all of the odds were against him Dr. Martinez replied, "I saw my parents working hard, day after day. But I never heard them complain. They would constantly encourage all of us to study, so that we wouldn't have to work as hard as they did." He stopped briefly to dry his tears, as he was painfully recalling his parents' sacrifice. "I love my parents very much, and I give them all the credit for my success. I thank God every day for them. They now live in a beautiful house in Van Nuys that I bought for them. Now they don't have to work anymore, since I provide for all of their needs. They were there for me every step of the way."

◆   ◆   ◆

Joe Gutierrez was the oldest of his three sisters and three brothers. His entire family had been born and raised in Los Angeles, and his ancestors had arrived there in the early 1900's. His ancestors moved from Guadalajara, Mexico, seeking a better life in America.

Joe was also a very bright young man, who excelled mainly in sports. In high school, he played football and baseball, and he was very popular. His family lived next door to the Martinez family. His father was a Los Angeles police officer and his mother was a bookkeeper. His parents were always trying to portray to everyone that they were well off. They bought nice cars, and took a vacation every summer. They wanted their children to have the best of everything. They gave them almost anything they asked for. They felt it was the least they could do for them. It really didn't matter to them what their children did with their lives, as long as they had money.

His parents saw the Martinez family as being very humble, and they figured the kids would be poor all of their life. Joe was Robert's best friend, and always liked to flaunt his new toys and clothes to him. His parents told him that he was "superior" than Robert, because he was an American.

Joe would always make fun of Robert for being so nerdy, and always worrying about getting good grades. He always saw Robert in the library and in the bookstores. He thought this was abnormal behavior, because a normal guy wouldn't do things like that. Joe had many girlfriends, and was the typical buff jock. He didn't see anything wrong in cheating on his exams. He figured after graduation he would become a police officer, like his dad, and then become the chief. He would use his father's influence to move up the ranks.

Joe was very unhappy about graduating from high school, since he would no longer have all of the girls that adored him. He would no longer be the star athlete that everyone admired. He struggled with the idea of attending college, since studying was obviously not his forte. He attended the first semester of a community college and couldn't go back. His parents never influenced him either way, and his father found him a job as a traffic clerk at the police department.

The years went by and Joe was now a senior traffic clerk in the same department. He was divorced, and had to pay child support to his ex-wife for their two children. He couldn't stay committed to just one woman, which was one of the causes of the divorce.

One day, he saw his old friend Robert when he came in to pay a traffic ticket. Seems like Dr. Martinez had gotten a little too excited about his new Porsche, while riding around town. Joe was shocked to see that Robert owned a brand new luxury sports car. He thought Robert must have been involved in some sort of illegal business. Since the Martinez family had moved out of the neighborhood a few years ago, he had lost contact with them.

"Joe, it's so good to see you after all of these years. I thought you'd be a police officer by now. How's your family doing?" asked Dr. Martinez with an excited tone.

"Robert, you look so different, buddy. It's great to see you. Look at you, you have a sophisticated look. Those students at Stanford sure had an influence on you. I've been working here for some time now, and I have to work overtime since I have to pay child support. Debbie and I got a divorce two years ago. It's been hell, man. I didn't think my life would turn out this way. I can see from the ticket that you drive a Porsche. Man, did you rob a bank or what?"

"Joe, you haven't changed. Well, remember all of the times you made fun of me for being so studious? Well, it paid off. After Stanford I went on to medical school, and now I'm a surgeon at the UCLA Medical Center. I have a lovely wife and two children. We live in Beverly Hills, and I bought my parents a home in Van Nuys, so they could enjoy their retirement."

Joe was momentarily stunned. This wasn't supposed to have happened. He remembers when Robert was dirt poor, and that's how he figured he'd be all of his life. What went wrong here, he thought to himself. His family was "better" than Robert's. But now the tide had turned.

"You know something, Joe. Every time you would flaunt your new toys and clothes in front of me, it caused me to become that more motivated to succeed. You felt sorry for me all of these years, but I felt more sorry for you. Your family fed you lies about how life really is. And now look at you. The once popular star athlete is probably stuck in a clerical job for the rest of his life. You should have come to the library with me, Joe, and maybe you would be driving a Porsche, too."

They exchanged addresses and phone numbers, and parted ways. Joe just couldn't see himself visiting Robert in Beverly Hills. He was somewhat jealous and confused. Now he knew the importance of getting a college education. It would be more difficult for him to go back to school at this stage in his life.

So as you see, in America anybody can make a dream come true. It just may take a lot of hard work and study time. But it will be so sweet once you attain it.

The All-Important College Education

One thing that I'm not particularly proud of, is the high percentage of high school dropouts among Hispanics. It is really a crying shame! I really don't understand this phenomenon. Why is this happening more and more each year among our young people? We are growing in numbers, but our education level is among the lowest in the nation. That is very embarrassing. Imagine what our nation will be like years from now if we don't improve this trend?

But even more appalling, and obviously not surprising, is our extremely low college graduation ratio. I want to hide behind a curtain, because this figure is really deplorable. How is it that we live in the land of opportunity where dreams come true and education is available to everyone, and we don't even take advantage of it? Now that is really, really absurd. I have not figured it out yet.

I do have a few theories, though.

Education starts at home, and the drive to continue studying comes from mom and dad. It doesn't matter what education level mom or dad has, it's their constant motivation to succeed that will keep us going. But the Hispanic family is in decline, since we have more single mothers raising their children, and are at the poverty level. They don't have time to develop their children, since they are busy making a living.

As long as we live in a materialistic society, where almost everything is within purchasing attainment, Hispanics will continue to remain undereducated. The credit card is the greatest of all evils among Hispanics. It is the cause of many devastated lives, and it has hit us hard.

So many times I have seen young Hispanics graduate from high school, and start working two jobs to buy a new car, new clothes, and other trendy items. They don't realize that these jobs will not last forever. But the debt they accumulate usually does. I feel proud whenever a young Hispanic that I have counseled pursues their college education. They soon realize they want a better life, and the only way to realistically reach that level is through a college education.

Of course, not everyone is meant for college. Others have skills that were once considered undesirable, but today are regarded in high esteem. One such profession is that of automotive technician. Today, a mechanic is referred to as an automotive technician, and he has to be familiar with computers, since most new cars have some sort of computer device inside. Many trained and certified mechanics today are making from $40,000 to $60,000, on average. This is a profession that attracts many Hispanics, and when performed adequately, it pays off in the long run. There are many other professions that today are paying better than before.

Parents, please take time to nurture your children and tell them at an early age the importance of an education. Whether it's to be a teacher, a nurse, an accountant, a doctor, a dentist, or even an automotive technician, just encourage them to pursue what they love best.

What It Takes To Succeed

1. Believe in yourself.

2. Seek encouragement from others.

3. Keep your focus on your dream.

4. Don't be influenced by the negativity of others.

5. Plan ahead effectively.

6. Become proficient in your area of expertise.

7. Seek advice from other successful people.

8. Take action and make your dream come true.

9. Don't forget about spending time with your family and friends.

10. Set aside time for your quiet moments alone.

11. Every day ask God to watch over you.

12. Live within your means.

13. Save money for the future.

14. Be a person of integrity, and treat people kindly.

15. Take good care of your health.

16. Don't get into any bad habits.

17. Share your ideas with others.

18. Avoid becoming proud.

19. Never forget where you came from.

20. Always be learning something new.

21. NEVER GIVE UP!

ENCOURAGEMENT

Find Joy in the Simple Things of Life

One Sunday, I was watching a cable channel that dedicates the entire morning to religious programming. On this specific day, they featured sermons by five religious leaders of different faiths, who pastor churches across America. The theme this Sunday morning was "simplicity."

It is an interesting topic, since we are living in one of the most materialistic eras of our time. People work hard in order to attain a big house on the hill, drive an expensive import car, wear expensive clothes, and vacation in exotic places. They feel these things will bring them true happiness.

In times when I am feeling down, I usually enjoy going to a bookstore and reading an interesting book. Usually it's an inspirational book that will give me the motivation to keep on going. I also enjoy the outdoors, and I like going to a park to walk, because I get to appreciate the natural beauty that God gave us. I love the sound of birds singing, the sight of the river or the lake, the beautiful flowers and trees, all looking spectacular because of the sun's radiating light. These are far more precious, and offer more satisfaction than what any material object can do for me.

We never know how long we will live in this life. If we spend the majority of our time here on earth accumulating wealth, and don't take time to focus on the simple things of life, we are cheating ourselves. God intended for us to be happy, and to be grateful for the world he created. How easy it is for us to forget that our life is a gift from God.

How easy it is for us to forget about the simple things in life. Start today, and focus on the simple things in life: read a book, take a walk in the park, call a friend you haven't spoken with in a long time, invite someone over for dinner, share your hobbies with others.

Find the simple things in life, and you will find contentment and a new purpose for living.

People

How really awesome it is to think
that God created people so different,
so diverse, but yet so beautiful.

I love to meet people every day,
it's truly my biggest motivation for living.
For in each person I see a reflection of God:
White, black, brown, yellow,
it doesn't matter what color they are.
It's the soul that's inside of them
that I care about the most.

I learn something new from
each person I meet.
A different perspective of life,
A different way to do things,
A different purpose for living.
People motivate me,
although they sometimes disappoint me.

How boring the world would be
if we were all alike.
I love to try new foods
I love to hear new music,
I love to learn a new language,
I love to discover a new culture,
I love to meet new people.

I thank God for creating the human race.
I am thankful that he created people.
I love people.

I Love To See You Smile

When you smile at me,
I feel so good about being alive.
You don't know how much it means to me.
I long to see you pass by me,
so that I can see you smile at me.

Your smile says a lot to me.
It shows the way you think of me.
It says that you approve of me.
It shows that you are happy,
when you smile at me.

The Noble Priest

When I owned my coffee shop, one of my regular clients was a Catholic priest. He had been a customer from my previous location in the mall. I remember seeing him walking around the mall every morning, as I was preparing the coffee. I didn't know he was a priest until he told one of my employees.

One day, he went to get his coffee but didn't know we had moved. He asked around, and was told we were in a new location behind the mall. He was glad when he found us. I was glad too.

I enjoyed the time I would talk with him, because I learned a lot from him. He taught me that you can be content being a single person. Of course, his vocation called for him to be single, since his whole devotion was to God. Regardless, it was how he focused on the positive and not the negative. He was raised Lutheran, and his parents were very disappointed when he told them he was going to study to become a Catholic priest. He said he knew all along that this was his calling in life.

He was leaving town to join a new parish in California, where he was originally from. He would be living with other priests there, and would be meeting most of them for the first time. They would become his new family. He would be starting a new life there. He never thought his life would take this turn. But he saw it as a mandate from God. He had served his time here, and now it was time to move on.

What I cherish the most was the advice he gave me. I was going through a difficult time, and I recall asking him to give me some direction. Having a business for the first time, I committed many errors. I was also the victim of employee theft, and employees giving out my secret recipes to a new competitor. I had a close friend who betrayed me, and I was deeply hurt. I was also going through financial struggles, and worrying about my future.

But I could count on him to be there every day. He would wait for me to sit in the same table so we could talk. Then he would thoroughly enjoy his cup of coffee, while listening to me.

He eventually moved away and came to bid goodbye on his last day. He would be driving from Texas to California all alone. Ironically, I did not know that soon thereafter, I would be closing my business and moving away as well.

I wonder how he's doing today. I know God is using him to minister to other people in his new parish.

Thank you for being a great listener and for giving me moral support. But most importantly, thank you for being a good friend.

The Lady Who Breathed Poetry

I remember the first time I heard her recite poetry. It was during a Sunday morning church service, and I was about twelve years old. She walked up to the pulpit and took a deep breath. First, she looked up and then closed her eyes. She held a book in her hands, and then she pressed hard on it. The moment was about to start. She was now transforming herself into a living poem. Really.

Then she opened her eyes, and looked intently at the congregation. There was silence. She uttered the first words of the poem with such fervor, that even the flies stopped to hear her recite. Her voice became loud, and everyone was mesmerized by the words that came out of her mouth. How did she remember so many verses of these poems that were so long? I recall that many of my friends found her very amusing, and couldn't help laugh. The next thing they would feel was their mothers pinching them hard on their legs, so they would stop laughing.

It seemed like this woman was possessed, as if she was crazy.

But yes, she was possessed. But it was the poem that lived in her. It was time for the poem to come out of her system, and be shared with others. And boy, what a sight it was. All of the poems were in Spanish, and most of them she had learned as a child. It was her Mexican father who had inspired her, and gave her this passion for poetry.

Through the years I became accustomed to her poetry, and I would look forward to her recitals: Mother's Day, Father's Day, Christmas, and Easter.

She has now gone to be with the Lord, and I remember the last time I saw her. For many years, she had a thriving business and had prospered much. Her entrepreneurial ability was another trait her father had left her. But she had no children, and her closest relatives had abandoned her in her old age. I took my mother and grandmother to visit her right before she died. They held this lady in high esteem.

She told my mother how tough the last years had been to her. She was ninety years old and still going strong. But I could see that she was lonely. But nevertheless, her faith in God kept her going on all of these years.

What an inspiration she had been to me, and she didn't even know it.

I can still hear her, breathing the poems, and enchanting the crowd. I will hear her for the rest of my life.

Every Day

Every day, be thankful because you have another opportunity.
Another opportunity to make yourself better.
You can enroll in a course that will improve your income and your life.
You can join a gym, and start working out for better health.
You can change your attitude, and new friends will come your way.
You can start saving money, for the down payment on a house.
You can start planning for the business you want to open.
You can take that vacation you always dreamed of.
You may just meet that special person.
You will make a difference in somebody's life.

Yes, every day is a gift from God.
He wants you to share your talents with those around you.
But don't wait until tomorrow to start.
Every day is not going to be forever.
Every day is today.

You Can Only Serve One God

A man from the Dominican Republic was visiting the United States for the very first time. He was here to attend a spiritual retreat, to be held in the Texas Hill Country. He came to learn different ways to get closer to God. He was a devout member of his local church in Santo Domingo. Poverty is prevalent in that nation, and the churches are full on Sundays. People look to the church for moral support and spiritual help.

After spending a few days in the retreat, and talking with some of the attendees, he was surprised at their way of thinking. Many of the attendees were immigrants from other Latin countries, while others were born in the United States. But, what stuck in his mind the most, was how many of them were not ashamed to ask God to prosper them. They claimed that God brought them to this country so they could make lots of money. They were trying their best to be right with God, so that he could bring them wealth.

The Dominican saw this thinking as so absurd and irrational. He knew this was the land of opportunity, but that didn't mean that God had to bless everyone by making them millionaires. He could only think of the poor people in his country, who lack all of the comforts Americans take for granted. His fellow Dominicans would be happy just to have a decent place to live, a car to drive, air conditioning, electricity, shopping centers, jobs, restaurants galore, running water, and grocery stores with a wide selection of food.

He soon realized, that the god who rules many Americans' hearts, is the god of money. Now, he could see for himself, why America was losing the moral values it was founded on so many years ago. People were only praying and pleading to God, to bring them material wealth, rather than spiritual wealth.

"It's harder to believe in God in America than it is in my country. All of my life I thought it was the other way around. You see, in America people have everything materially that we lack in our country. Yet, Americans aren't satisfied. They want more. An average American would be considered rich in my country."

"I will return to my country with a new attitude. I will tell my congregation that we may not be rich materially, but we are so much richer spiritually than Americans.

We can only serve one god, and I choose to serve the one and only God. For he is the one that gives me everything I need."

We are rich and we don't even know it.

Take some time to reflect on what you really value the most in this life. Become a servant of the one true God. He has given you what you have today.

You Are Special Indeed

You are a mixture of different races.
How marvelous you look.
You are the way you are because that's how God wanted it.
Don't compare yourself to anyone else, because you are you.
There's no one else in the world like you.
You have a unique soul.
You have a unique mind.
You have a unique spirit.
You are unique.
Therefore, you are special.

The Secret for Living a Happy Life

It seems these days everyone wants to sell you
the secret for living a happy life.
For thirty-nine ninety-nine you too can have it.
Then, you are disappointed after you buy it and find
there's no happiness, when you realize you've been tricked.
But, happiness is not something that's for sale.
It's one of God's gifts that is free, as he says in his Word.
But we focus so much on having material possessions,
and about getting ahead in this life and acquiring wealth.
And there's more to happiness than these things.

So, how can you be happy in a world that is in such turbulence?
First, you must accept and love yourself as you are.
God made you his way for a reason, and only he knows why.
Then, you must love those around you, and show them that you really care.
You will be astounded at the amount of love that you will receive in return.

Then, you must eliminate worry from your thinking, because
things will happen, and you will be able to overcome any obstacles, no matter
what.
Accept whatever stage in life that you are in, because you will grow stronger.
Never compare yourself to anyone, because you are unique, and have special gifts.
Remember, you will only live once in this life, and you want to enjoy it fully.

Give thanks daily, whether things are good, or whether they are bad.
Talk to God everyday, because he will listen, and he cares about you.
Once you die and reach eternity, you will meet God face to face, and you'll be
surprised
to see that you knew him all along, and will be with him forever.
Then you'll know why you were so happy in this life!

Special Moments and Things We Cherish

The birth of a baby

The baptism of a baby

Our first communion

A Quinceañera

A mariachi band

A midnight serenata

A daughter's wedding

High School graduation

College graduation

A cruise in the Caribbean

The beaches in Mexico

Sipping a margarita

A trip to Disney World

Eating our traditional Hispanic foods

The aroma of our favorite foods

Mexican tamales in Christmas

Lechon asado on Christmas Eve

Spanish turrones during the holidays

Grapes on New Years Day

Mexican enchiladas

Jalapeño Peppers

Empanadas

Pupusas

Ceviche

Arepas

Tacos

Cuban Sandwich

Tres Leches cake

Flan

Café Cubano

Going to Miami Beach

A boat ride on San Antonio's River Walk

Going shopping in Mexico

Finding a dream job

Getting a promotion

Buying a house

Buying a new car

Buying new clothes

Listening to romantic Latin ballads

Listening and dancing to Salsa music

Listening and dancing to Tejano music

Attending a concert by a Latin musician

A barbecue

Cascarones in Easter

Seeing a Latin star in person

The first grandchild

The support of family and friends on the death of a loved one

The extended Hispanic family

Seeing our children succeed

Being proud of our Hispanic heritage

Sharing special time with your friends

Drinking hot and spicy chocolate on a cold day, the kind abuelita used to make.

Taking a walk in New York's Central Park

Shopping at La Placita Olvera in Los Angeles

Fiesta time in San Antonio

Calle Ocho in Miami

Having lunch with friends

Family gatherings

Our parents' advice

Relaxing with a café con leche

Our school years

That first kiss

That special love

Our traditional clothes: Guayaberas and Mexican dresses

Our sons and daughters coming back from war

OUR FAMILY

The Hispanic Family

One of the greatest things about being alive is being able to share your life with those that are closest to you: your family.

What is surprising to non-Hispanics is how extended the Hispanic family is. The traditional American family consists of the father, mother, children, and grandparents. In today's corporations this is what is classified as family, for bereavement purposes. But to the Hispanic, the family consists of many more individuals. It includes uncles, aunts, the in-laws and relatives of the in-laws, first cousins, second cousins, third cousins, and so on. We consider many people as part of our family. We don't want to be lonely, so practically everybody we meet becomes our family.

For those of us who have been somewhat "Americanized", we still secretly long and cherish the time spent in family reunions. We may not want to admit that we're like those "recent arrivals", but we are. We can't deny that. It's part of who we are, and we have to feel proud of that. There's absolutely nothing wrong with considering many people as our own. It's really a beautiful thing.

I was speaking to a friend the other day, and she mentioned how close her "family" is. She said when one of her sisters, brothers, or cousins, is going through hard times they all take turn in helping them meet their needs. She said they don't even think twice about it. To her, all of them are her blood relatives, and she enjoys helping them in their difficult periods. She can't understand the traditional American family. She said most Americans don't know that they are depriving themselves of the joys of the extended family. She would have it no other way.

It is a beautiful sight, whenever I see a large Hispanic family gathering. Everyone seems to be having a good time, and everyone is genuinely concerned about each other's family and welfare.

Take pride in the fact that you are part of a large family, people who value you and love you for what you are. Never lose this sense of family, and never be ashamed to admit that you truly consider them your loved ones.

You can never erase the memory of the special times shared with your family. They will keep you coming back for more new memories.

The Mother:
The Force Behind Every
Successful Hispanic

One of my favorite success stories shows how important the mother is in our Hispanic traditions. I came to know one of these special mothers, and saw how every single child became successful in their own respective ways.

Her husband was an immigrant from Mexico, but he had attended school in the states. In college he majored in a specialized engineering field, and later found work as an entry-level manager in this area. He met his wife in college, and knew that this woman was very special. They got married, and she was the force behind his career, motivating him to progress. And, she encouraged him when things weren't going so well.

They had four children, and he felt thankful to have attained a managerial job, that was helping provide for his family. A few years later he became the president of the company, and suddenly the family's social status changed for the better.

His wife was also the main force behind the success that each of her children would attain. She knew how difficult it had been for her husband and her to reach this status. She didn't want her children to go through these same struggles. She had a strong faith in God, and she instilled this faith in her children as well.

Their oldest daughter is a now a high school teacher. Their oldest son is a medical doctor. Their middle son is an engineer, like his father. And the youngest son has had a successful banking career.

Just like this special woman, my mother was also the force behind our family's success. She would constantly be after us to finish our homework, and to stop watching television. She would visit our teachers, and find out from them how well we were doing. I was the "smartest" of her children, and she wanted me to become a professional some day. Although I did reach some milestones, I didn't quite become the professional that she so wanted me to be.

But mother, I can still hear your words of encouragement as I write these stories. I hope to make you proud someday, and finally reach the status you so wanted for me. I know you are watching me from heaven, and making sure I don't deviate from the path you taught me. You are the force behind all of my success.

Mother

◆

A Tribute To My Mother

How truly beautiful is the love of a mother.
There are not enough words to describe this unique love.
My mother was a very special lady.
I feel blessed having had a mother like mine.
I could not have asked for another one.

Thank you God for choosing this precious woman to
be not only my mother, but my friend and guide.
I will always remember her sweet smile.
I will forever cherish her telephone calls to
see how I was doing.
To make sure I didn't lose courage.
To tell me how much she loved me.

I can still feel her presence, for she
will never leave my side.
I can still hear her words of wisdom and love,
and they will stay with me forever.
I am who I am today because
of the love of my mother.
I know that I will see her again someday,
and this gives me the strength to go
on living every day.

Dear mother, I will always love you!

My Mother's Words of Wisdom

I lost my mother last year, but she will always live within my thoughts and my heart. What I will treasure most is the wonderful advice she gave me, whenever I was going through struggles, or having to make important decisions. Most Hispanic mothers care about the well being of their children, no matter how old they are. They will always be our mothers, and they want the very best for us. They are always there to welcome us with open arms. Please cherish those moments that you spend with your mother. She may not be the smartest woman in the world, but she loves you more than any person in your life. God bless all mothers.

1. Don't pay attention to what others may say about you. Everybody is a critic. Only you know what you want, so don't let others influence you negatively.

2. Be careful that *envy* doesn't bring you down. People will always want what you have, or what has taken you much sweat to attain. Just keep focusing on accomplishing your dreams.

3. Be punctual in all of your appointments. It brings you respect.

4. Always keep your commitments, and you will be seen as a person of integrity.

5. Never seek revenge, because it will only lead to self-destruction. Learn to forgive, and it will bring peace of mind, and cure a broken heart.

6. Don't get into anybody else's business. Let people live their life according to their own standards. Let your neighbor live their life the way they want, so long as it doesn't interfere with yours.

7. Don't try to please everyone, because sooner or later you will be disappointed. Focus on financially helping those closest to you only. If you lend money, don't expect to get it back, since not everyone has the same values you do.

8. Your appearance says a lot about you. Always look your best.

9. Take time to relax your body and mind, before making an important decision.

10. Remember that your family will be there for you always.

Ode To Their Migrant Worker Dad

One night, I was listening to a national radio program that features a popular female disc jockey. The listeners call in with their requests, and tell a story of why they want to dedicate a certain song.

On this evening, a very educated young lady called in her request and dedication. She told the disc jockey that she wanted to dedicate a special song to her father, for all of his hard work. Because of his sacrifice, she had just recently graduated with a Masters degree in Education. Her two other sisters also graduated from college, and one even has a Ph.D. They all attributed their achievements to their poor father, who toiled day and night, so his daughters could succeed in America. He didn't want his daughters to be migrant workers like him.

The caller started crying tears of joy, and she said how much she loved her father. She can now share the fruits of his labor with him. All of his daughters bought him a house, and this is a special tribute since he raised them as a single father. Their mother died when they were little girls, causing them to mature at an early age.

She asked the disc jockey if she could address her father in Spanish, since he had never learned to speak English well. And there, on a national English-language radio show, the caller dedicated the song to her father in Spanish.

Papi, I just want to tell you how much I love you. I want to thank you for what you did for me and your other daughters. You don't know how proud we are of you, and how we thank God for having a father like you. I know it was hard for you raising three daughters on your own, but look at how well you did. I want to dedicate this song to you on national radio, to show everyone how much I admire and love you. Thank you papi, for everything you've done for us, and for making us believe that we could succeed. God bless you.

This prompted the disc jockey to respond in her broken Spanish *"Que Dios bendiga a tu Padre" (May God bless your father)*. She then played "Wings Beneath the Wind" by Bette Midler, for her father.

What a beautiful way to express gratitude for everything her father had done for her and her sisters.

And what a beautiful message it was to the nation, of how a poor Hispanic father was able to raise three successful daughters.

Thank God for America!

I Can't Believe We Just Ate That Pig

I probably shouldn't tell this story, but I feel compelled to share it. Since it involves my father (who is deceased) and another good friend of his (who is still alive) and has a great sense of humor, I feel safe in telling it.

It was Christmas Eve 1982, and we were living in Austin, Texas. My father and his friend had been toying around with the idea of roasting a pig, for the sake of keeping our Cuban traditions alive. My father was the pastor of a small church, and he had a member who had a farm and owned some pigs. Well after some talking, the next thing I know is that this farmer donated a pig to our family. My father had explained to him how Cubans celebrate Christmas Eve by eating a roasted pig. The next day I woke up to find this big, fat pig outside of our house and next to the church. The minister's house was located next to the church, making it convenient for us to walk back and forth.

Since Christmas Eve fell sometime during the week, there were no scheduled church events. The Christmas program had been held the Sunday before. We were just praying that no one would find out that this pig was tied next to the church. My father's friend, another minister, came over early that day with his wife. It was going to be a special occasion for both families. My father and his friend were raised in farms back in Cuba, and they had plenty of experience in killing pigs. But I asked him whether it was legal to kill a pig in the city. He just pretended not to have heard what I asked him, and proceeded to kill it.

It was a much more simple process than what I had expected. I witnessed how they took the pig's life, and I will spare you the details. The pig squealed very low, so the neighbors didn't hear it.

The next task was up to my mother and our friend's wife. They helped in cleaning and cutting the meat, and preparing it to be roasted. They marinated the pig with bitter orange, *mojo* (a Cuban marinade), garlic, pepper, onions, and olive oil. When it was finished cooking, we all gathered at the table and gave God thanks for the wonderful meal. It was the best Christmas Eve dinner I have ever had. The thought of eating the pig that had been there just a few hours ago was repelling at first. But after tasting the finished product, it was well worth it. We also had the traditional *congris* (black beans and rice cooked together), yucca, and plenty of desserts.

The wonderful thing was that a divorced man, who had just recently started attending the church, showed up. He had not spent the day with his family, and we invited him to have dinner with us. He tasted our style of cooking for the first time, and he ate like there was no tomorrow.

What wonderful memories I hold of my time together with my parents. This is one of those that I treasure, since I laugh every time I think about it.

Father

✦

A Tribute To My Father

My father was a magnificent man
who was intelligent, articulate, and spiritual.
His calling as a minister led me
to live a very exceptional life
He longed to see me follow his footsteps.
But my heart led me on to different
paths in life.

He was more than a father.
He was also my best friend.
I can only imagine how much
he suffered when he decided to
bring our family to the United States.

Thank you God for giving me a father
who didn't give me material wealth.
The wealth he left me is far greater than
that which money can buy:
He gave me the secret for living a happy life.

His passion for poetry I can now say I share.
For I will never be as great a poet as he.
But I will honor him with my simple poetry.
For then I can proudly say that he certainly
left me a most rich legacy.

A Proud Father

His son was just eight years old when he started playing baseball.
The father wanted his son to be an athlete, just like him.
Many times the son would hear his father tell him stories of days gone by.
"Son, you should've seen me when I would get to the plate.
There was no way of stopping me. I hit so many homeruns that I lost count
already.
I was the star of my high school baseball team. How I miss those days."

His father would take him to the little league practices and watch his son's
progress.
The father would always encourage his son, even when he didn't play well.
He attended every single game that his son played in.
He was his son's biggest fan and the son knew it.
He loved his dad for being so supportive.

The son also became a high school baseball star.
But unlike his father, he won a baseball scholarship and went on to college.
His father couldn't attend college because he married young.
He had to work two jobs to provide for the family.
The son became a baseball star in college, too.
His dad drove to see every single game. He was so proud of his son.

The son graduated from college and got drafted into the major leagues.
His father saw him play whether in person or on TV.
His son had received a million-dollar contract.
The son played for many years and later retired.
He founded a chain of restaurants and prospered even more.

Finally, the day came when the father was dying, and the son was full of grief.
His biggest fan in life, the man who motivated him to succeed, was now leaving
him.
"Dad, I love you so much. I could have never asked for a better father. I am who

I am today because of you. You supported me all the way. I'm gonna miss you,
papi."

"*Mi hijo*, God brought you into my life so I could have happiness.
I always thought I was a failure. All I excelled in was sports.
After high school I had to grow up fast, and life was bitter for me.
But then you came along. My whole world changed after that.
Thank you for giving me such good times.
Promise me that you will support your own son, the way I did you.
I want him to bring you the joy that you brought me.
Carry on the tradition, my son, because
I want you to be happy for the rest of your life. I love you, son."

With that, the father closed his eyes and died.
The son wept. He was distraught.
His eight-year old son was next to him and gave him a hug.
"Dad, I'm gonna make you proud. I'm gonna miss grandpa, too.
But I don't want you to be sad.
I'll be there for you always, just like you were for grandpa."

The son hugged his own son, and cried both tears of sorrow and of joy.
He was now a proud father, too.

The Wedding Day

Her mother was so full of emotion.
Just seeing her daughter looking so beautiful made her cry with joy.
She remembers when she brought her into the world.
How happy she was to be the mother of a cute baby girl.
She would see that baby grow up to be a woman.
And now, this was her special day.
The bride knew what her mother was thinking.
She too was happy, since she had found love.
Her mother gave her the best advice, and she thanks God for her.
The traditional Hispanic customs, that her mother taught her,
made her what she is today.
She will continue these traditions with her own children.

The groom waits impatiently in the church.
He can't believe the day has finally arrived.
The girl he fell in love with so many years ago will now become his wife.
She motivated him to pursue his education, and now he's a professional.
His father and mother are very proud of him too.
They saw their son grow up in a different world than theirs.
They gave him everything they never had while growing up.
They were able to prosper by starting their own restaurant.
That's how they saved to send their son to college.
They feel blessed at having such a wonderful daughter-in-law.
They love her like if she were their own daughter.
They know she will make their son very happy.

They exchange their vows and kiss.
They are now man and wife.

The reception is held in an exclusive country club.
A mariachi band surprises the couple, and sings to their love.

Everyone toasts for their future life together.
They ride off in an exotic white limousine.

Their new life together as one has begun.

GRIEF AND DISAPPOINTMENTS

Life Without You

I didn't know if I would get used to it.
I thought I would feel lost not having you around.
You were a major part of my daily life.
I took your presence for granted.
I got so used to you being by my side.
I thought you would be with me forever.
I was shocked, numb, and upset when
you were taken so suddenly away from me.
You didn't warn me that you were leaving so soon.
I didn't get to tell you how much I loved you.
I didn't get to tell you how much you meant to me.
Now I only have the memories of the times we shared.
I only have things that remind me that you were once a part of me.
I only have pictures of the wonderful times we had.
I guess a new chapter has started in my life.
It's feels so weird, so bizarre, not having you around.
I only wonder what life without you is going to be like.

Dealing With Grief

One of the hardest moments in life is whenever we lose someone that is dear to us. The first time I experienced this was when my father died. He had been a minister most of his life, and he had been my role model. I remember, as a teen, how he would ask me to sit with him in the dining room table, and we would talk about different subjects. He really wanted me to become a minister, too. He saw how committed I was to church events, and how I had a good sense of what was right and wrong.

Unfortunately, growing up as a minister's son I got to see the human side of my father. I also saw how people would call him at all hours, because they needed his moral support. It could have been a wife whose husband was abusing her, a son who wanted to run away from home, a father who was unemployed and needed to put food on the table, a disagreement between two members of the church, or simply someone wanting to get to know God better. He did all of this, and yet the salary was so low. But he always had enough money to feed and clothe us. I really admired him for that.

During his last days he was bedridden, suffering from the symptoms that cancer had brought into his body. I couldn't understand how God had allowed him to suffer in this manner. He had committed his whole life to serving God, and I thought it was rather unfair that he would die this way. But we don't know why God allows certain things to happen. I remember him telling me in Spanish when I was about fifteen, "We have to accept things for what they are. We should never question why things happen. Our brains cannot understand the "why" of things. Don't overload your mind with thoughts that perturb you. Think only of those things that you understand, and you will be in peace."

The hardest thing for me was seeing how my father died, with only my mother on his bedside. The doctor had not emphasized to us that he would be dying soon. My mother was devastated, since she had complete faith that the chemotherapy would keep him alive for many years. She was very dependent on my father, as is customary with Hispanic women of her generation. For the first time in her life, she found herself all alone without the man she loved profoundly. I still hear my father talking to me and giving me advice. Whenever I am going through a difficult period, I close my eyes and envision talking with him. He still gives me excellent advice.

The next deaths in our family came in less than a month from each other. I lost both my grandmother and mother three weeks apart from each other. We were expecting our grandmother's death, since she was ninety-one years old, and had Alzheimer's disease. We had made the difficult decision of placing her in a nursing home. Slowly, she started losing her memory, and her health condition began to deteriorate rapidly. She died seven months later. My mother was her only child, and once again she felt devastated.

My mother had health problems of her own, but she was an introvert. There were certain things she kept from us, and she had not told us that she was feeling ill herself. Together, with feelings of disappointment at seeing my business fail, my brother's and sister's personal struggles, and now her own mother's death, she kept it all inside. My mother had heart problems, and had been diagnosed with blocked arteries. I had taken her to a specialist, and he recommended she have a special surgery to unblock the arteries. The problem was my mother had lost faith in medicine after my father's death. In essence, it almost seemed like she had given up. She lived five years after that diagnosis, and we were told she suffered a stroke. I remember calling the ambulance to come pick her up, and I thought how it had all come down to this. She stayed in the hospital for two weeks. I remember well her last night, when we got the call from the male nurse that her condition had taken a turn for the worse. I knew it was coming. We were losing our mother. Gosh, we hadn't even had the time to recuperate from our grandmother's death.

My sister, my brother, and I all stood around her in the intensive care unit where she had been all this time. We held her hand and we were crying tears of sorrow. We would never see our mother again. It had all happened so quickly, and with no previous warning. How could we have known that we would lose both my mother and grandmother on the same year, and in such little time?

But we tell everyone that witnessed our family's ordeal that there is only one thing that kept us strong and at peace: our faith in God. The one gift that our parents and grandmother had left us was having introduced us to God through his son Jesus Christ. That is the only thing that has kept us going all of these years. We know we will see them all in heaven one day. But for now, I know they want us to go on with our lives, and to live it fully. That's why they sacrificed their own lives to come into this nation, so that we wouldn't have to suffer the way they did. They had done it all for us.

It has been a year since I lost both of these women. As I look back, I thank God for honoring me by bringing them both into my life. They are my inspiration for writing, and for spreading love to everyone with my simple words. We will all die one day. But for those of us who believe in eternal life, death is only the beginning. The best is yet to come.

I Thought You Were My Friend

The first time we met, we had so much in common.
It was as though we'd known each other for such a long time.
We became good friends, and shared many great times together.
I learned a lot from you, and you learned a lot from me.

We both wanted so badly to have successful businesses,
so we helped each other in various ways to make this happen.
I introduced you to people who became your clients,
and you helped me set up my business, and made it appealing.

We had plans to work as partners, since we trusted each other.
Or so I thought, until you betrayed our friendship with a foolish act.
You lied to me, and you disappointed me by being dishonest.
I don't understand how you could have done this to me.

I was so proud of what you had accomplished in such little time.
I even said you were like a brother, and welcomed you into my family.
But you were only using me, since you knew I had many contacts.
And all you wanted was to make lots of money, no matter what it took.

I felt so stupid, and so irate, since I thought that certainly
there were still decent people living in this confused world.
It hurt when I realized that you were nothing more than a con artist.
That you had taken me for a fool, and you didn't care at all how I felt.

It took me a long time to get over your betrayal, and it left a negative mark.
I am now very skeptical of people I meet, and I have doubts about them.
But I don't understand how there's people like you in this world,
who pretend to care for others, who enjoy fooling people like me.

I hope someday you find peace within yourself. Because that's what you're lack-
ing.

75

You don't care about hurting people, because you have been hurt many times.
I tried my best at showing you the path that would lead you to success.
But you didn't want to listen. You accused me of being righteous.
So you have chosen to take the path of destruction.

Good luck, my friend. I hope you change before it's too late.

How it hurts when someone you hold in high esteem suddenly betrays you. I don't understand it, because it's not in my nature to be that way. Unfortunately, it happens often within our Hispanic culture. I think I've learned my lesson.

I Need You

If you only knew how much I need you.
I long for your touch, to hear your voice.
I desire your love. I hunger to see your face.
I need you to be by my side, near me.
Please understand that I can't live without you.
The thought of losing you is driving me insane.
But did I ever really have you?
Do you feel the same about me?
I need you, I need you, I need you.

How beautiful, but yet how bittersweet this thing called love is.
When you are no longer loved it's so painful.
We all need to feel loved.
It's in our blood.
It's in our soul.

Nobody Calls

I lie on my bed all alone,
and wonder why I feel so down.
There's no ring from the phone,
and there's so much to do in this town.

So, why is nobody calling me tonight?
Haven't I been a good friend and guide?
I guess I'll lie here on another lonely Saturday night,
and just read, or watch TV, until the night has died.

How horrible it feels when your friends have forgotten about you.
Don't they remember all the good things you've done for them?
How could they be so cruel?
I hate feeling lonely.

RICH, FAMOUS, AND HISPANIC

Gloria Estefan

I had been a fan of Gloria Estefan, since the days when she sang in Spanish with the Miami Sound Machine. I memorized all of her songs, and bought all of her record albums. I was proud of her accomplishments in the Latin music world, taking a mixture of Cuban and American sounds, and creating a new rhythm for everyone to enjoy. Her music made me proud of my Cuban roots, and I immediately identified with it. I always wondered what my life would have been like had I grown up in Cuba, or in a predominant Cuban community. She was a part of my generation, and her songs were indicative of all of the young Cuban-Americans, who were trying to find themselves in this new country.

In 1984, I made the decision to move to Miami to get to know my Cuban roots. I had planned the trip for a year, having visited Miami with my father and brother in 1983. After that trip I knew I had to move there. I loved learning about my culture, and seeing the success that the Cubans had had in America in such a short time. It was not easy getting used to the Miami culture, since I had to learn many things. I held two jobs to make ends meet. In the morning I was a bank representative, and in the evenings I had a part time job in the newly opened Saks Fifth Avenue in Dadeland Mall. I worked seven days out of the week, but I was enjoying meeting new people, and learning more about different cultures.

At Saks, I worked in the fine chocolates department, and before then I had never heard of paying thirty dollars for a pound of chocolates. I grew up with Hershey's, and that was just fine with me. Many celebrities walked through the store during its opening weeks, and it was exciting to see them. But seeing Gloria was the most impacting of them all.

One day, I was standing behind the counter talking to two other co-workers: Pilar, an older Mexican lady, and Annie, a young Cuban-American girl. We all felt so proud of working in such an upscale store, and we were discussing our experiences with customers. Suddenly, I saw a short woman come into the department, and she started browsing through the gift packages. I stared intently at her, and I almost fell over. It was her! It was Gloria Estefan! I didn't know what to do. I was excited, but nervous at the same time.

I turned to Annie and said to her "Look, there's Gloria Estefan."

"You liar. Where, I don't see her?" she responded not believing a word I said.

"There, that lady that's standing right there, by the gift packages", I whispered to her.

Then we saw Emilio, her husband, come and stand by her side. He said something to her and walked off.

"See, that's Emilio."

Annie's jaw opened, and now she knew I wasn't lying.

"Oh my God, it is her. Pilar, look that's Gloria Estefan and her husband Emilio."

Pilar didn't think it was a big deal, since she probably wasn't familiar with Gloria, or her music.

The next thing that came to my mind was how was I going to introduce myself, without invading her privacy. Obviously, she was out shopping with her husband, and the last thing she needed was to be hounded by a zealous fan.

I finally made my way over to her, and politely and nervously asked her, "Ma'am, is there something I can help you with?" How stupid of me, why couldn't I have just told her I knew who she was, and that I was glad I had the chance to meet her in person? But no, I had to pretend that I didn't know who she was.

I was shocked at her response.

She looked at me, and she simply walked away, without saying a word!

My favorite female pop singer had just been standing there in front of me a minute ago, and now she was gone. I couldn't believe it. But it was my fault, for not being brave, and letting her know that I knew who she was. Nevertheless, I got to see her face to face, and I would still continue being her number one fan.

A few months later *Conga* hit the airwaves and it was an instant hit. I remember how many times the Miami radio stations played it over and over again. Gloria and the Miami Sound Machine had made the *crossover* from Spanish to English. Then came many other hits after that, and the rest is history.

Whenever I hear her music from the 1980's, it brings back many wonderful memories. I not only adored her for her music and for her natural style, but also because she was my inspiration for succeeding in America.

I was shocked and saddened when she went through her horrible accident. I plead with God not to take her away so soon. How could her success end up like this? It wasn't fair. She had so much ahead of her.

Like millions of other fans, I kept myself updated with her progress. How happy I was to learn that the operation had been a success, and that soon she would be touring again. I was part of the crowd for her comeback concert in the Miami Arena. I enjoyed the night thoroughly, and I felt more connected to her.

But I will never forget that initial encounter with her. She gave me the motivation to believe in myself, and to make my dreams come true. Her singles *Reach* and *Always Tomorrow* are personal favorites that I frequently listen to when I need my spirits lifted.

Thank you, Gloria, for your music and your devotion to helping improve the image of Hispanics in our nation and the world. I just finished hearing your new CD *Unwrapped,* and watching the DVD that your son Nayib made. I can identify so much with you. It makes me proud of my Cuban roots.

You are an inspiration to Hispanics of all ages. You have given us hope for succeeding in America too.

Selena

✦

Taken Away Too Soon

I was at a Chinese restaurant in San Antonio, located right across from Selena's boutique, on the day she was murdered. I remember it distinctly.

I was eating lunch with a co-worker when he heard the two ladies behind us talking about Selena's murder. He was repeating to me what he was hearing them say, but I couldn't believe it. I told him they must have been talking about someone else. But he kept insisting it was Selena they were talking about.

Much to my surprise, when we exited the restaurant, television reporters were already gathered on the outside of her boutique. I then realized that it was true. Selena, the famous Tejano singer, was dead.

I recalled how only the previous month I had seen her performing on television at Miami's *Noche de Carnaval* event. It was her first international presentation on television, and she was a hit. After her performance, a famous Spanish TV entertainment reporter interviewed her, and I remember how relaxed she looked. She knew this was one of her most important performances, and she was superb. The reporter asked her to describe her style of music, since it was new to many listening to it for the first time.

There was a great chemistry between her and the reporter, and she was continuously smiling and laughing. He was also trying to understand this style of music that had not been marketed so heavily before. It was evident Selena was already a star. Her humility and her remarkable personality won over many new fans that night.

I was proud of Selena because she was determined to introduce her brand of music, Tejano, to the world. She was proud of who she was, and what she sung about.

We will always remember Selena and her music for as long as we live.

But her death was also very significant to the Hispanic world in other ways.

- The nation witnessed the thousands of people who attended her funeral. Most of these who were there were Hispanic.

- Many Americans wanted to know who Selena was, since she obviously touched many lives prompting many to travel from far away cities, just to be at her funeral.

- It opened America's eyes to the burgeoning Hispanic population.

- Jennifer Lopez, who portrayed Selena in the movie, was the first Hispanic actress to be paid one million dollars for a movie role. She has since become one the leading actresses in Hollywood.

- Selena's new album reached the top of the Billboard charts right after her death. Music companies witnessed first-hand the power of the Hispanic market.

- Her death made many young Hispanics proud of their heritage, their culture, their music, their traditions, their Spanish surnames, and themselves.

- Her life was an example of believing in a dream, and sacrificing many things to be able to attain it.

Selena will always be remembered as a person who inspired many to succeed in this great country of ours. She will forever have a special place in our hearts.

Music

Oh how I love music,
all types of music.
It's one of the most wonderful
things about this world.

Music makes me incredibly happy.
But it can also make me cry.
I love salsa, jazz, country, easy listening,
love ballads, Latin songs, rock, soul,
dance, and inspirational music, too.

It's so interesting how one song
or one melody can make me
feel really good about being alive,
and about being myself.
And how another song can make
me feel incredibly sad.

Nevertheless, I need music,
because it's my favorite form of therapy.
It inspires me to do my best.
It gives me hope for finding true love.
It motivates me to write.
I love music, and music loves me.

Sandra Cisneros

✦

Our Famous Writer

I had heard about this famous Latina writer, and was not quite familiar with her work. A friend who is an English professor introduced me to her writings. One day, while chatting with her, I mentioned how there were so few renowned Latino writers. That's when she mentioned the name Sandra Cisneros.

I had heard about Ms. Cisneros because she had been in the local San Antonio media lately. It was about the controversial color she had chosen to paint her house: purple. It had caused a stir in her neighborhood, since she lives in a historic area. When all of this was going on, I was not interested in the literary world or writing. But that whole situation stayed on my mind.

I actually got interested in writing right after my mother's death. I had written her life story and read it during her funeral. It was a very emotional time for me, and I had to stop several times to prevent from crying. I received many compliments afterwards about my writing, and I knew that somehow I was going to write more and better.

A few months after my mother's death, I had breakfast with my friend again, and she told me about an upcoming literary festival. She said it was partly sponsored by Ms. Cisneros, and other authors would be there as well. She sent me the festival's catalog, and I made plans to attend a few of the events. The highlight would be the night when Ms. Cisneros would read an excerpt from her new novel *Caramelo*. When I owned my Italian coffee shop, I allowed a group of poets and writers to have a similar reading. That was my first exposure to an event like that. Thanks to two of my employees, Monika and Alejandra, whose love for literature convinced me to hold this event.

The night of the reading, I went with a friend that I had recently met at another book signing. He was also in the process of writing a book in Spanish. When Ms. Cisneros took the stage everyone in the audience became calm. She briefly described the chapter she was going to read from, and received a standing ovation at the end. Everyone then proceeded to go to the reception area, where books were also going to be sold, and Ms. Cisneros would be signing copies of her books. I chose to buy *The House on Mango Street,* because the story had touched me. With all of the excitement, I somehow ended buying the Spanish version. It really didn't matter since I can read Spanish fluently.

The line to have the books signed was long, and when it was finally my turn to meet her, she was very kind. She was displaying a brand new tattoo on one of her arms, which goes along with her radical personality. When she took my book to sign it, she noticed it was in Spanish and said, "You read Spanish? That's interesting!" She proceeded to sign her name and I thanked her.

She didn't realize how she had inspired me to become a writer. But I'm sure many people have told her that. Although, I don't always agree with some of her writings, it's her freedom of expression that motivates me more.

La Sandra, as she is known in literary circles, is the best example of how a poor Latina girl believed in her dream and became a famous writer. And Sandra, it really doesn't matter: Latino or Hispanic, we're all the same. May you enjoy many more *exitos* and *aplausos.*

When I Met Jorge Ramos

♦

The First Time I Attended an Author's Book Signing

I had seen him on television for many years, anchoring the national news on the Univision network. I remember the first time I saw him on television, as the co-host of a popular daytime show on the same network. The next thing I know is he has been promoted to the anchor of the network's newscast. In Spanish we have a saying that says *"Quien le dio la palanca?"* (Whom did he know that gave him this job?) In the Hispanic culture, influential people tend to help each other out. It is an acceptable fact, in all of the Latin countries, that you have to be rich or know someone who is, to move ahead.

Nevertheless, after reading Jorge's book I was surprised that he didn't come from such a prominent family. His success was the result of hard work and personal sacrifice. We can see that he enjoys his work as a television journalist, because he immerses himself in the stories. Through him, we have seen a different angle of reporting stories, than that presented by the other networks.

It was just a few days before his appearance that I found out about it. It was to be held at a San Antonio Barnes and Noble bookstore on a Saturday in November 2002. I was one of the first ones to get there, and he hadn't yet arrived. A store clerk told me the only way to see him was to purchase his book. I knew that he was there to promote his book, and he wanted people to buy it. But I didn't realize that you had to buy the book in order to see him. I wasn't planning on buying the book. I was just interested in seeing him in person, and hearing what he had to say.

Regardless, I purchased a book and I stood in line. The crowds started arriving shortly thereafter, and the line was soon going out of the bookstore, and into the sidewalk outside. I met so many people waiting in line, and it was interesting to hear everyone's story of why they were there. One lady said she admired him very much, even though she didn't speak Spanish fluently. She was learning to speak

Spanish, and she enjoyed seeing him read the news. Another lady was a huge fan and she brought him a bouquet of flowers.

I saw how people would finally get to meet him, and talk to him as if they were the best of friends. Many flashbulbs were going out at once, since many wanted to have their picture taken with him. As I was getting nearer to him, a lady approached me, and asked me to hand him over a special note. She told me to tell him it was from a dear friend, and to point towards her, and he would recognize her.

When my turn finally came I shook his hand, and I gave him the note, and pointed towards the woman. He recognized her, and they exchanged a few words with each other. I had my picture taken with him, and I felt honored standing next to him. Here was one of the most influential Hispanics in the nation, who is a role model for many of us. He came into this country with nothing more than a dream, and has achieved the success that many Americans wish they could have. He told the crowd the story of his visit to Houston, promoting his book. Apparently, the bookstore wasn't expecting so many people, since they had never heard of him. They had never seen so many Hispanics there before. It was a wake up call to them, signaling that the Hispanic consumer has purchasing power, and needs to be attended to.

The one thing I remember most about Mr. Ramos was how he humbled himself in front of the crowd. He made them laugh, and he made them cry. And he told them he wasn't leaving until he signed the book for the last person waiting. That really showed true professionalism, and a sincere devotion toward his fans.

Bookstores—My Favorite Friends

My favorite thing to do when I feel bored
is to head straight to visit a friend—a bookstore.
Whoever came up with the concept of the mega-bookstore
should be awarded a special Pulitzer Prize.
I have my choice of so many different locations for either
Barnes and Noble, and Borders, and I enjoy going to all of them.
I usually have a topic in mind, and then I select a book and sit down to read.
I may spend hours there until I finish the complete book.
And if I don't, I remember the page I left off at, and return to
finish it on another day.
Of course, if a book interests me a lot, I buy it.
Otherwise, I'd rather read it at the bookstore, and spend some quiet time there.
Sometimes, I stop by the coffee shop and order a latte
or a frozen drink. My favorite is Starbuck's caramel Frappuccino.
I enjoy reading non-fiction as well as inspirational books.
But I also like different types of fiction, and poetry, of course.
If I have time, I head towards the magazine section, and I
give my eyes and my mind a much-needed rest.
As I stroll through the travel section, I think of taking a vacation.
When I glance through the automobile magazines, I dream of owning an exotic
car.
And when I get to the writers' magazines, I browse through almost all of them,
for then
I get really inspired, and I feel proud of my minor accomplishments as a writer.
Then, I go into the music section and I look for new material.
If I see a CD that I like, I try to listen to it first before I buy it.
Music is so relaxing.
I feel at home when I am at a bookstore. It's like visiting a close friend.
The beauty of it all is that I always look forward to my next visit, because I get to
visit another friend at another location. I know where everything is, and I

like the uniqueness of every store.
Thank you bookstores for being such excellent friends!

The Cristina Show and My Attempt at Stardom

There was another main reason why I had moved to Miami, besides getting in touch with my Cuban roots. I wanted to become a TV star! It didn't matter whether I was making commercials, or if I was the weatherman on the local Spanish news. I just had to be on television.

During the 1980's, Miami had emerged as the new capital of Spanish TV, and for sure I knew I had the talent to succeed. Unfortunately, I got my welcome to reality. I wasn't aware that many others had come to Miami with the same dream. And most of them had more experience than I did. This was not fair, I thought. I was even booted out of an ad agency that was responsible for producing the majority of the commercials in Spanish. This happened after I decided to introduce myself to the agency's staff, and I made plans to visit them one day.

When I got there, the wife of an old Cuban actor, who was the talent manager, greeted me. I told her who I was and that I was interested in acting in commercials. She looked at me with a look that said, "how dare you have the audacity to just walk in here, and think you were going to get an acting job". "Who sent you here? Whom do you know that told you to come here?" she said in a very condescending tone of voice. I simply replied that no one had sent me. I had just read that this agency was where most of the Spanish commercials were produced, and I wanted the chance to audition for one. She abruptly told me that I needed to go through a casting agency, since that's where they got most of the talent. I found that hard to believe, since most of the same actors appeared on all of these commercials. I felt like a puppy whose behind just got whipped by its owner. I still didn't give up.

After that experience, I signed up with a talent agency, and certainly now I knew I would get an audition. But, the only "big break" came when one of the agents called me, and told me I would be cast as "the man with the hat", in a video that Don Johnson was filming in Miami Beach. I was ecstatic! My big break had come. I was going to be in a music video with the star of *Miami Vice*.

She told me what to wear and where to report. I felt like such a star. Finally I had been discovered, I said to myself.

I arrived and parked my car in a nearby parking lot. I could see the production crew setting up, and I saw many people who obviously were taking part in the video. I got closer, and I had never seen so many weird people before in my life. As I got to the front, I saw a lady who looked to be in charge, and I told her that I was "the man with the hat". She didn't particularly seem to care, and then told me that all of the "men with the hat" were standing over there. Wait a minute, you mean there were other men with the hat? I felt depression hit faster than a bullet hits its target. I had been fooled again. Or maybe, I had fooled myself again.

I got to see Don Johnson in person, and the filming lasted until 2 o'clock in the morning. By then I was tired, and I wanted to go to sleep. I didn't want to participate in something where I wasn't even guaranteed a small role. I wouldn't be noticeable with so many "men in the hat". I remember walking off the set during a break and I heard someone yelling in the background, "Hey, where are you going? The filming isn't over yet." Well, it was over for me. I vowed never to do this again. This was a very humiliating experience, and I certainly didn't want to do it just for fun.

My "big break" actually came when the *Cristina Show* was started being televised on the Univision network in 1989. The show's producers invited the bank staff, where I worked, to attend a taping of one of the shows. The specific show that we went to dealt with people who had posed nude for art's sake. I was just excited to be a part of the taping of the show. I didn't want this moment to go to waste, so when the portion of the show to ask questions came, I stood up and asked one. I don't remember what it was, but it made it to the final cut. I was finally on TV! And on national television at that. Later on, I found out through my parents that many people had seen me.

We were invited back to participate for another taping, and this time the topic was about people who were considered attractive. I remember how I had the question memorized that I would ask the guests. Then to my surprise, one of my co-workers who was sitting next to me, was chosen first and asked that very same question. What was I going to do, I was next with my question? Out of the blue, I asked one of the guests, "Do you have a need to be constantly told you are attractive?" and she answered, and so did every single one of the guests. Once again I was on national TV, and the camera took a few shots of me while asking the question, and as the guests were answering it. I received many phone calls from people who had seen me. People from as far away as California and Texas commented that they had seen me, and how good I looked. That's all my ego needed—a good boost.

Cristina Saralegui, the show's host, was very personable and I didn't realize the show would become the success it is today. It has become a true example of someone who achieved the American dream. Just standing next to her, I felt that she was transmitting her success vibes into my body. After that experience, I promised myself that I would pursue a career in television.

I moved back to Texas in 1991 and I took several communication courses. I was able to obtain a news internship, with the San Antonio Telemundo station, and I shadowed the female anchor for a semester. I used to practice reading the teleprompter before the newscast, and I dreamed of someday being an anchor.

That dream wouldn't come true until I moved back to Laredo, Texas where I had graduated from high school, and vowed never to return. It was there that I had decided to start my gourmet coffee business, since there were no other businesses like it. That summer, I saw an ad for a new morning show co-host and I sent my resume, and the station manager called me for an interview. We found out that we had both graduated from the same high school, and she saw how excited I was about the job.

When I had my audition, it was in both English and Spanish, she was more surprised at my fluent Spanish. She immediately told me I would be anchoring the 5pm Spanish news, as a guest anchor for two weeks, until the main anchor recovered from an illness. The two weeks turned into two months, and I became a local celebrity. Months later, I accepted a job as a reporter for the English newscast, but had to resign soon thereafter due to personal reasons.

For a period of six months I had lived my dream and I knew I had the talent to succeed. I just wished this had happened years ago when my dreams were more vivid, and my motivation was stronger.

Do I see another television job in the future? I want to become a motivational speaker, and the answer is yes, since I can reach more people. But I don't see myself in television news again. But the experience made me believe in myself, and in my self worth.

We Have Finally Made It!

I was a customer service supervisor in a San Antonio cable company for many years. My ultimate goal was to eventually become a part of the Public Affairs department, but that never happened. The politics of the corporate world once again prevented me from advancing in my career.

Nevertheless, I was able to change my economic situation for the better during my time there. I was sacrificing my career to be closer to my mother and my family. It's a Hispanic thing—to want to be close to your relatives. I probably could have landed a higher paying job somewhere else, but I chose to stay nearby.

One of the perks of working for the cable company was being able to meet famous people. I met George Foreman, Morgan Fairchild; two leading actors from the HBO series *OZ*; the wrestlers *The Million Dollar Man* and Sean Michaels; Ralph Emory, host of *American Movie Classics*; and the fitness guru Jake Steinfeld, who gave me a free copy of his book, *Power Living,* and signed it "Ruben, Don't Quit!"

But, the ones I fondly remember are our Hispanic stars. The first one I saw was Paul Rodriguez. The minute he walked in everyone couldn't help but laugh. He is obviously a comedian and people expected to laugh with him. What struck me the most was how really down-to-earth he was. He was joking with the employees, who were mostly Hispanic, and making them feel as if he were their friend. He showed us that his celebrity status had not made him feel better in any way. He's a true star!

Maria Conchita Alonso also paid us a visit. It was part of the publicity campaign for her new talk show on the Telemundo network. She was wearing a short dress and she seemed somehow tired. I'm sure she was traveling to the different markets where the show would be transmitted. She started talking about her life, and mentioned that she was born in Cuba, but raised in Venezuela. At that comment someone mentioned that I was Cuban, and she turned to see me and said "Oh, but you are a Cuban-American, since you were raised in this country." That comment surprised me, because coming from a fellow Cuban it felt strange to be categorized as such. The more I thought about it, the truer it became. I was a Cuban-American. I could not be one without being the other.

Meeting beautiful, famous women is not my habit, but it seems I was given plenty of opportunity to meet many of them. Three of these come to mind. Laura Herring, Odalys Garcia, and Sofia Vergara.

Laura Herring was co-hosting a show on VH1 when she paid us a visit. Many years had gone by since she had been crowned the first Hispanic Miss USA. I remember watching that pageant, and since she was representing Texas, it made me proud that such a beautiful girl was chosen to represent American beauty. And she is a very beautiful Mexican-American girl.

I briefly talked with her and told her I remembered when she was crowned Miss USA, and she replied "Gosh, that was a long time ago. I can't believe you remember that." But how could I forget, Laura. She was just as beautiful as the day she won that pageant. Many of the younger employees didn't remember her as a beauty pageant winner, but they recognized her as the star of a recent dance movie. Boy, how time flies fast, and how soon things get forgotten.

I met Odalys Garcia at the Texas Cable Show that is held annually in San Antonio. I had seen her on TV as a co-host of a candid-camera type of show. Her beauty was striking in person. The line was long, full of guys wanting her free calendar, and her autograph. When it was my turn, I approached her and told her I was a big fan. I told her I was proud that a beautiful fellow Cuban girl, like her, had found success in such a short time. She asked me what a Cuban was doing living in San Antonio, and I laughed. She gave me her calendar and signed it, and we took a picture together, and I asked her for a kiss, which she kindly agreed to. It was a sweet kiss and a sweet moment for me. No other guy attempted to ask her for a kiss, and those around me congratulated me on my boldness.

The other Hispanic beauty that I had the chance to meet in San Antonio was Sofia Vergara. She was here to promote the opening of a new Bally Fitness Center. The line was huge to get her autograph, but a friend and I managed to work our selves inside. Since we were on our lunch break we couldn't afford to wait. We made our way upstairs where she was located. We squeezed through everyone, and got closer to where she was. And there she was, sitting down, looking more beautiful than a Greek goddess. We got close enough to admire her beauty, and boy was she ever stunning. It was well worth having sacrificed lunch to come and see her.

I felt so proud at these three beautiful women, because they had actually accomplished what very few Hispanic beauties had done in recent history. They proved that Hispanic girls are beautiful, and that they don't have to forget their culture in order to succeed in America.

I remember growing up with names like Farrah Fawcett, Marilyn Monroe, Jaclyn Smith, Cheryl Ladd, Bo Derek, and Heather Locklear. But now here are Laura Martinez-Herring, Odalys Garcia, Sofia Vergara and Maria Conchita Alonso. Four Hispanic bombshells who are very proud of their Hispanic heritage and kept their Spanish names. Unlike previous Hollywood starlets, who were forced to change their names, they kept theirs.

Now we have successful actresses like Jennifer Lopez, Salma Hayek, Cameron Diaz, Patricia Velasquez, Jessica Alba, Elizabeth Peña, Lauren Velez, and Penelope Cruz, who are just as proud of their Hispanic roots, and their names.

And we can't forget the Hispanic actors who have kept their Spanish names:

Edward James Olmos, Andy Garcia, Ricardo Montalban, Esai Morales, Mario Lopez, Antonio Banderas, Eduardo Verastegui, Benicio Del Toro, John Leguizamo, Paul Rodriguez, George Lopez, Raul Julia, and movie director Robert Rodriguez.

What a positive change for all of us who were ashamed to admit our culture so many years ago.

Watch out, Hollywood, because here we come!

You're An Angel On Earth

✦

A Tribute To Jaci Velasquez

You are such a beautiful woman.
You don't know how lovely you really are.
Your beauty is not only external, but internal too.
The delicate manner in which you express yourself.
The high moral values you have kept throughout your life.
How could you remain so pure, so sweet, so fresh in
a world that is so rotten and so confused?
You stand high above all other women, for you
are a woman of righteousness, who has wisdom and an honest heart.
The world looks at you and they don't understand
what makes you so different from the rest?
But I know the reason why you shine brighter than the sun.
It's because you are an angel on earth who God is
using to show others His love.

As a Christian and a Hispanic, I am very proud of Jaci. She is truly the best example of a Christian celebrity who has kept her moral values. I have followed her career from the time she came on to the Christian music scene with her phenomenal hit "Un Lugar Celestial". She got the Anglos to start singing in Spanish. Hallelujah! She is always proud to stand for her faith in God and he is richly blessing her. Now she is having success in the Latin music scene and also in Hollywood. Jaci you are most definitely an angel here on earth.
Que Dios te siga bendiciendo mucho!

LOVE

Love Comes When You Least Expect It

Pablo had been lonely for about five years now. He couldn't believe he was going through this loneliness, at this stage of his life. His marriage was supposed to have lasted forever. How could she have left him for another man? What was she thinking of? She left him with two young boys who soon would become teenagers. The thought of raising them alone was too much for him to handle. With his low teacher's salary, he was forced to maintain his household as best as he could. He consumed his time mostly at work, and spending as much time with his kids. Surely, no other woman would want to marry him, especially now that he had two boys. He took long walks in the park every day to forget his misery.

His closest friends were worried at his sudden change of attitude. They didn't want to see him suffer this way. They asked God to work a miracle in his life, and bring a woman who would love him and care for him. They had complete faith that this would happen.

One day some friends held a party at their house and invited Pablo to come over. They told him to bring his boys too since it was a family type of party. They had also invited Cecilia, who was a registered nurse, and had been single all of her life. Cecilia was a beautiful woman who had been courted by many men. But she just hadn't found the right one yet. Until that night.

The moment they were introduced to each other it was love at first sight. They looked intently into each other's eyes, and knew there was something special between them. He introduced her to his children, and she liked them too. The kids thought she was very pretty and kept hounding their dad to marry her.

The courtship lasted for about six months until Pablo proposed to her. He was the happiest man alive when she accepted. They held a lavish wedding in her church, and then an extravagant reception in a beautiful country club. It was the happiest day in her life. A love story, who brought two people who were born in two different Latin American countries, and found each other in America. She was born in Peru and he in Puerto Rico.

It's been seven years since their marriage, and now they have a handsome young six-year old son. The two young boys are now teenagers, and they love their father, their adopted mother, and their new brother very much.

Love stories still happen, even in our modern times.

Your Parents Must Have Really Been In Love

Your face is such a work of art.
Everything seems to be in the right place.
The shape of it, your luscious eye brows,
your beautiful eyes, your perfect nose, your succulent lips,
your precious smile, your ideal chin, your illustrious hair,
the way you speak, the way you walk, the sophisticated way you look.
There's only one explanation for this:
Your parents must have really been in love,
and God blessed them with you.

Hispanic men are famous for their *piropos*. These are poetic sayings that are frequently told to beautiful women as they pass by. Often they are crude, but I chose to use only words that edify and describe the beauty of a woman in my *piropo*.
This *piropo* is dedicated to all the beautiful women in the world.

She Gave Love Through Her Cooking

Everyone who knew her was aware that she had led a very rough life. Both of her ex-husbands had abandoned her. One of them had physically and mentally abused her. She had raised her two children alone, and she almost didn't make it. Sometimes, she recalls the times when she didn't have money to support the family. She had to place her pride aside, and ask her relatives and friends for financial support. She had developed a low self-esteem, and thought about committing suicide on various occasions. But there were always people around her, who offered encouragement, and the motivation to go on living.

What I remember most about this woman was how giving she was towards others. She didn't realize the wonderful talent she had in cooking. I recall how she told me she only knew how to cook in large quantities, because that's how her mother had taught her. Many times she would end up throwing food away, because she had cooked for about eight people. I encouraged her to bring the left over food to work, since I knew many people were going through financial hardships themselves. How grateful these people were whenever she brought this food. She, in turn, told me how grateful she was that I had suggested that she do this.

One Christmas she invited me over to her house to enjoy her traditional *menudo. Menudo* is a Mexican style soup, containing hominy and other ingredients. She had made this meal for about twenty people, and she wanted me to be one of the lucky ones who got to try it. How good it made me feel to see how I had helped her change her attitude about her life. It was the best *menudo* I had ever had.

Forbidden Love

I see you and I ask myself, "Why can't I have you?"
I know our love would be so perfect, so complete.
I would love you like I've never loved anyone before.
I don't understand why there are laws
that are getting in our way.
Preventing us from sharing our love for one another.

I know you feel the same way
about me as I do about you.
I know it by the way you look at me.
I can see it in your eyes.
But we haven't had the chance to be together,
since we're both afraid of the consequences that
showing our true feelings would cause.
So we go on living, waiting for the day,
when we finally will be able to express our love.

Sometimes we fall in love with someone who already belongs to someone else. Unfortunately, we have to suffer the consequences that come along with having made this choice.

Lovers

They left the famous San Antonio bakery and headed for the River Walk. They parked at the Rivercenter mall's parking lot, which is adjacent to the River Walk. Blanca loved to stroll through the shops. Pedro was in awe seeing all of these shops and the tourists passing by. Everything looked so modern, and being with Blanca made it that more special. He had never seen such an elaborate place back in Mexico.

Blanca wanted him to experience the boat rides. She purchased their tickets and they waited in a long line until their turn came. They got on the boat, and the tour guide began telling them about the river's history, and how it tied into the city's history. Pedro looked over to glance at Blanca.

A cool breeze passed between them. She got closer to him since she was feeling chilly. He truly was enjoying this special moment.

The boat passed through the outdoor restaurants, and he saw many people having lunch. He didn't realize that the river walk was so romantic. He imagined he was in Venice. Blanca told him that they would have lunch at one of these restaurants, and it would be his choice.

After the boat ride they walked back to the restaurant area. Pedro chose a restaurant that served typical Texas food. They sat down to order a meal that consisted of Texas-sized steaks, baked potatoes, cornbread, and a salad. He loved to eat steaks, so this was a special treat for him. Blanca was treating him today, so he was splurging. They sat outside by the river walk, and they watched people go by. They saw many boats passing by full of tourists. They would wave every time one of these boats passed by. He noticed there were people from all over the world visiting the river walk. This would become of his favorite places to hang out. He was truly having fun. Something he hadn't done in a long time. He was finally in a fancy restaurant dining with a decent woman. If only he could live this way and experience it every day.

They finished their meal and now Blanca wanted to find out more about Pedro. She wanted to know who this mysterious man was. He was so adventurous and had such a free spirit. Surely he must have had an exciting life full of different types of experiences. She wanted to know if he had left a family behind.

She wanted to know if there was a special woman in his life. She wanted to know how he became so well mannered and educated. She was about to find out more about his life.

"So, Pedro, I want to find out more about you. First of all, where were you born?"

Pedro looked at her knowing full well that this was eventually coming. He knew she was intrigued by him and wasn't going to stop until he told her about his life. He didn't want to keep anything away from her. He would reveal some of his most intimate secrets to her. He knew she would be so fascinated by these, that she would have no other recourse than to fall more in love with him. Was he falling in love with her? This had only happened to him once before. He didn't believe in love again after that painful experience.

"I was born in Saltillo, but I was raised in Mexico City. I never knew my father. He doesn't even know I exist. My mother never talked to me about him at all. In fact I didn't know my mother very well either. My mother was an alcoholic and she saw me as a burden. I reminded her of my father. She was in love with him but he didn't feel the same way. She told me once that I looked a lot like him. I was a constant reminder of that lost love that she was trying so hard to forget."

"I was always a good student and the teachers recognized that. One of my teachers saw how my mother was ignoring me. In fact it probably qualified as child abuse. My clothes were always dirty and I hardly ate. I still don't know how she got money to buy liquor, but there was none left for food. Some of the neighborhood ladies would feed me from time to time."

"But I just learned to live without food. I would drink lots of water and grab some fruits from the surrounding trees." This was painful for Pedro since he was not used to talking about his personal life. He had learned long ago to refrain from showing any emotion.

Pedro continued telling Blanca that with that teacher's assistance he was awarded a scholarship to a Catholic boarding school for the poor in Mexico City. This special school existed because of a nun's dream. Sister Maria knew that the country had a high rate of kids who lived in poverty. She wanted to change that. She wanted to give those kids a chance to succeed in life. It took her many years, but she was able to convince the government to establish this school.

With Sister Maria's efforts many wealthy families in Europe helped support the school. Each child was in turn sponsored by a family. With their money they were able to buy their clothes and books. The Brandenburg family, from Germany, was Pedro's sponsor throughout his years at the school. He never met them, but he named his carpentry business after them, as a gratitude for what they did for him. Pedro's eyes were watering as he was recalling his painful childhood.

Blanca was getting emotional listening to his story. Now she knew why his business had that name. She was looking intently in his eyes, and she wanted him to go on with the story. She could visualize everything he was telling her.

"I lived in the dorms until I graduated. My classmates became my immediate family. Some of them went to Europe after graduation, to meet their sponsors. Many of them stayed there and are very successful. The school has produced many doctors, attorneys, and entrepreneurs who are now helping to support it financially. We all consider Sister Maria our adopted mother. She was always very encouraging to all of us."

He told Blanca how the school was up to par with all of the upper class private schools in Mexico. They studied the same materials, and were taught the proper manners and etiquette necessary to be successful in life. He loved to sing, and he won the school's talent contest one year. He was twelve years old, and sang an old romantic song. He was so happy. His prize was a brand new pair of shoes. It was the best thing that had ever happened to him.

Tears were coming down Blanca's cheeks. This story was much too moving and she could not contain herself. She could not imagine what it would be like to grow up without either your mother or father.

"I always had an aptitude for working with my hands. I was artistically inclined but I knew I wouldn't be able to make a decent living being an artist. I loved to paint and I my paintings were always attracting many people's attention. But, as you know, in Mexico it's hard to make it in that field. It doesn't matter how good you are. So, I had to find my niche and that's how I got into carpentry and construction. At fifteen, I helped build many of the schools' new buildings. I designed and planned them myself. Sister Maria and the school staff were in complete amazement at my abilities."

"I knew she had a special place in her heart for me. I could see it by the way she treated me. You don't know how much I love that woman. She is truly a gift from God."

Pedro continued relaying his story. He told Blanca how he dreamed of owning a huge construction company in Mexico. He got a taste of this when he was assigned to head the construction of some housing projects, when he was only seventeen. He was paid well for this and he learned to save and invest his money. This was something Sister Maria taught all of the students. He also learned to be very independent, because once he left the school he would be on his own. Since he never had a real family, he was very indifferent towards family events and holidays. He learned not to trust anybody and to rely only on himself. He took life one day at a time. He also told her how he studied this art of cabinetmaking, with a renowned cabinetmaker from Italy. He immediately knew that this was his ticket to success. He would combine both his artistic and construction skills to create beautiful cabinets.

"So what made you come to the United States?" asked Blanca.

Pedro wanted to keep certain things to himself. He didn't want Blanca to know every single detail of his life. He still didn't know how far his friendship with Blanca would go.

"Well, as you're well aware, Mexico's economy hasn't been good these last years. For a while I built cabinets for the rich in various cities. I was getting referrals left and right. The problem is that the wealthy there are very tight with their money. They don't take my profession seriously. They see me as a laborer, not as an entrepreneur. I took the jobs because I had no other way of making a decent living. But they were getting away with murder. I don't even want to tell you what they were paying me. I had always heard that America was the land of opportunity and many of my classmates had already come here. For many of them it was hard making it, but others were able to find jobs. I decided I was going to America to make lots of money. I would then be able to return to Mexico and start my own construction company. And you know that the process for getting visas is not easy, so I came into the country with a temporary passport. It has since expired and now it's harder to apply for the new laser visas. But now that I'm here, I don't want to go back."

Blanca still had doubts about his full story. Did he have a wife or a girlfriend? Surely a handsome guy like him had to leave someone behind. She now knew why he was so well educated and cultured. But she wanted to know more about him. What was his true motivation in life, and where did he see himself in the future? What did he think about love and did he ever expect to get married? But she also wanted to know how many women he had loved.

"Have you ever been married, and do you have any children?"

Pedro stared straight into her eyes knowing what kind of answer she wanted to hear. He couldn't help smile since he found the question silly at this point.

"No, to both parts of your question. I didn't want to be tied down while I was pursuing my dream. I've had many women who I shared special relationships with. But I never let them lead into anything serious. I'm not ready for marriage just yet. I want to be able to provide my future wife and family with a decent lifestyle."

His answer was to the point, but Blanca still thought that he was a *Don Juan*. She didn't really think he was ever going to get married. He was enjoying this stage in his life, since he was good looking and charming. He would probably remain this way for several years. She didn't think he'd be able to be loyal to just one woman. *He must have many other secrets that he wasn't going to disclose to her?* But she would eventually bring them out of him.

They continued talking for a while, and then Blanca suggested they visit other attractions that were close by. She didn't want to ask too many questions today. She would slowly find out more about this mysterious man who had come unexpectedly into her life.

They visited the Alamo, which is a shrine commemorating a famous war between Texas and Mexico. They went up to the Tower of the Americas, and then walked through the city's historic downtown area.

The rest of the week Blanca made her daily stop to see Pedro. They continued talking about his many loves. They also talked about his dream to start a construction business. Now he wanted to have that business in San Antonio. They talked about literature, the many books they had both read. He taught her how to make the fruit smoothies that he drank daily. She bought him some new clothes and shoes. All this time they were just talking like good friends. Not once had either one of them made an attempt to kiss the other. They were just enjoying each other's company. It was a nice change for both of them, especially for Blanca. This was the closest to a fantasy that she had ever gotten. Being with another man and sharing intimate secrets with him was beyond her wildest dreams. Pedro longed to see her more and more everyday.

Blanca's family was very wealthy, and her father was very strict. He was a widow and had not had luck in love again. Blanca had become very attached to him after her mother's death. She knew her father would be strongly against her relationship with a recent immigrant. It would be a scandal for her prominent family. She had met and fallen in love with Pedro when he was contracted to remodel their kitchen. He was the most handsome man she had ever met in her life. Late one night Blanca called Pedro. She wanted to talk to him, to hear his voice.

"Hi Pedro. Did I wake you?"

"No, it's okay. Are you all right? You sound worried?"

"I'm fine. My father hasn't arrived home yet?"

"He doesn't allow me to be an independent woman. But where is he tonight? Is he with another woman? It's just not fair, that's so disrespectful of him. He's already forgotten about my mother."

"You're worrying too much, Blanca. Your father is a grown man and he has the right to seek happiness too. But if I were your father, I would be just as protective as he is with you. Men would do anything to have a woman like you. I hope you're not offended by what I just said? But I want you to know that I'm here whenever you need someone to talk to. You are the most beautiful woman I have ever met in my life."

"Thank you for being so understanding. I don't believe I'm doing this. I'm actually calling you and divulging my personal problems. Please forgive me. I don't know what's wrong with me. But thanks again for being so understanding. I'll see you tomorrow. Good night."

Blanca hung up the phone before Pedro could reply. He just stood there and knew that soon Blanca would be his. She could no longer restrain from hiding her true feelings for him.

The next evening Blanca made her daily visit to Pedro's apartment. She wasn't her usual self. Tonight she had a worried look. She had been wondering where her father had been last night. She needed to feel that someone loved her and cared for her. She needed to feel the arms of a man wrapped around her body. She needed to hear a man tell her how beautiful she was. She needed to be with a man who wanted to be with her. She was finally going to succumb to Pedro. The timing was right and her defenses were weak.

When Blanca walked in, she stood there staring at Pedro. He noticed there was a different look in her face.

Something was troubling her, and her whole body was shivering. He walked over to ask her what was wrong, and found himself wrapping his muscular arms around her. This was the first time they had ever embraced. He saw tears building in her eyes. She told him why she was feeling this way. He wiped the tears softly away from her eyes. He knew the moment had come. This was the perfect opportunity to declare his love for her. His large hands took her face and held it gently. He first kissed the tip of her nose, then her eyes, and, finally he satisfyingly kissed her soft mouth. Pedro's kiss sent new sensations of ecstasy through her entire body. She kissed him passionately, savoring every moment.

Pedro was more in love with Blanca, now that she was his. From now on nothing was going to stand in their way. Their lives would never be the same again. They would live only to give each other love and pleasure.

Blanca was speechless lying there next to Pedro. She had never experienced this kind of love and passion before.

Pedro had made her feel like a complete woman.

Blanca had never felt so fulfilled and happy. She didn't want this moment to end. *How could she have been so deprived of a love like this?*

"Blanca, I am so in love with you. I thought I would never be able to fall in love again. But you have proven me wrong. *Te quiero mucho. Te adoro. Haz llenado mi vida de gozo y amor. Eres todo para mi.* You are everything to me."

They continued kissing throughout the night. They had both found true love.

I'm Still Searching For True Love

I can't believe the years have flown so fast.
It seemed like it was only yesterday
when I discovered this thing called love.
I have fallen in love many times,
but it wasn't love at all.
It was only my imagination playing tricks on me.
For in my dreams I have loved many times,
and I haven't been hurt by any of my lovers.
When I wake up from these dreams, and face another day,
I feel lonely, abandoned, unaccepted and betrayed,
because my imaginary lovers don't feel the same about me.
Oh, how I long to have someone love me and care for me.
I can't help but feel envious when I see two people in love.
Especially people who have been together for a long time.
I'm still searching for my true love, if in fact there is one.
Until then, I wake up every day hoping, and waiting, and praying.

Can we still find true love in today's world? It's been so hard for me, since I am a true romantic.
I want to find true love. It's much more than the physical. It's the spiritual qualities of a woman that will eventually win me over.
Can someone help me find true love?

I Wanna Get To Know You

I can't believe it finally happened.
You have fascinated me since I met you.
And there I was standing next to you, close to you.
I finally got to see your face, your hypnotic eyes.
I got to hear your voice, and see your lips.
I gave you the chance to look at me, to notice me too.
And now I think about you all the time.
Sometimes I can't sleep because I want you beside me.
The thought of you with someone else is killing me.
Please give me the chance to get to know you,
so you can get to know me and need me too.
I want you to love me, the way I love you.

Love Crosses Borders

Alma can never forget the first time she laid eyes on Roberto. Her prayers were answered the day fate had them meet.

When Alma was twenty years old, she worked as a waitress at one of Caracas' finest country clubs. She was so beautiful that her beauty immediately captivated every man that saw her. Many of them were married. However, in Venezuela it is tradition for these prominent men to have mistresses. She was asked continuously to consider becoming a mistress. The offer usually included a luxurious apartment, a maid, travel throughout the world, and lots of spending money. Had it not been for her strict religious upbringing, she would've probably already accepted one of these offers. But she remembered her mother's advice: *Always give yourself respect and dignity. Love will eventually find you.*

One day, while serving drinks in the country club's pavilion, she saw a very distinguished man sitting in a table by himself. He looked to be in his mid-thirties, and was short and slender. He had black hair and brown eyes, and a nicely trimmed mustache. She walked over to offer him a drink.

"Good morning, *señor* what can I get you?" Alma said, as she was accustomed to.

"*Buenos dias señorita*, you are a very beautiful girl. I could not help noticing you from a distance. You are very elegant and I can tell you had a good upbringing. What is your name?" He said as he continued smoking his fine Cuban cigar.

"Thank you for the compliment, you are very kind. My name is Alma," she responded politely.

"Ah, Alma. I can tell that life has been good to you. Your face radiates an air of freshness. It's too early for a drink, so how about getting me a glass of fresh orange juice and some cookies." His eyes were fixated on her face. She, in turn, was feeling somehow different about him than the other men who tried seducing her. She sensed he was being honest with her. She started wondering whether this was the man she'd been dreaming about all of her life.

She came back in a few minutes with the orange juice and the cookies and set them down on his table. "*Gracias*, Alma. Please have a seat so we can get to know each other better. I would be very honored to share this time with you."

"Oh, thank you *señor* but I can't do that because I am working right now. But I do appreciate your kindness and hospitality. Maybe we can plan to do that on another occasion. Is there anything else that I can get you?"

"You are so beautiful, and so polite, and I know it's the way you naturally are. And my name is not *señor*, it's Roberto…Roberto Del Mar. I want to see you again Alma, before I return to Miami. Where can I reach you so we can plan to meet again?" Alma was hesitant to give him any of her personal information since she did not know who he was.

"I have a better idea, I get off at four o'clock every day. Why don't we just plan to meet for an afternoon *merienda* in the little bakery that is down the road from here? They have Caracas' best pastries, and the best cappuccino you can find anywhere."

He was amused at her suggestion, but he knew he was falling in love with her. "That sounds like a great idea, but since I leave tomorrow evening, can we plan to do this today?"

At first, she hesitated since she was used to turning down these types of offers, but then said, "Certainly, as long as I get home by six o'clock, otherwise my mother will start to worry."

"Don't worry, I assure you that you'll be home by then. I will pick you up at four in front of the country club."

"Oh, no Roberto, that's not necessary. I'll walk and we can meet there, if it's alright with you?"

He smiled because of her naïve demeanor. "Okay Alma, I will be waiting there for you."

"Thank you, Roberto for your invitation, and for respecting my decisions. I'm not used to riding with strangers, even though I know you are an honorable person. I will see you then." As she was leaving, Roberto knew immediately that she would become his next wife.

◆   ◆   ◆

Her shift was over, and as she was getting ready to leave, Alma felt uneasy about meeting with this stranger.

She could hear her mother's warnings in the back of her mind. Nevertheless, she said goodbye to her fellow workers and headed for the bakery. Around this time, she'd be heading to the bus stop to catch the next bus that would take her home. Dolores, her mother, knew that whenever she was late, it was because she was either out window-shopping, or at the grocery store.

When she arrived at the bakery, she was surprised to find that Roberto was already there. He had reserved a table for them towards the back of this small place. It was a very romantic setting, since the ambience had a touch of Paris. As she walked in, she could see and smell the French bread, and the fine pastries. Soft, romantic music was being played, and the smell of freshly brewed espresso filled the room. A tray full of fine pastries lay in the middle of the table. The owners, an older couple, were happy to see her, and hugged her as she walked in. They didn't know she was the special guest that the distinguished gentleman was waiting for. Roberto got up and kindly escorted her to her chair and she sat down. "*Gracias, Roberto. Usted es muy amable.*" The waiter brought her cappuccino to the table.

"You have great taste, Alma. This little place reminds me of the cafes that I visited in Europe. The coffee is superb and the pastries are the best I have ever had."

"Why, thank you. I am happy that you like it. I often come here to relax, and I dream of being in Paris or Venice. It's my time to get away from it all. And the owners are like a second family to me. Sara and Raul have had this bakery for over thirty years. They modeled it after a bakery they visited in Paris on their honeymoon."

"I love to hear the beautiful stories about their travels. Sara always tells me that one day I will get a chance to travel around the world."

"Oh, please take some pastries. I didn't know which kind was your favorite, so I ordered a variety. I tried the eclairs and the guava pastries, and they are simply irresistible." Roberto looked intently at Alma's beautiful eyes.

"Everything looks so good, you didn't have to be so generous. I think I will try this cheese danish, it's such a big portion. I think you ordered too many of them. I won't be able to finish it all."

"That's perfectly fine. Whatever is left we will have them placed in a box, and you can take them to your mother. Do you have any brothers or sisters?" asked Roberto.

"Yes, I have a younger sister and she loves to eat pastries. I watch my weight, so I usually limit the amount of sugar I take." Alma took a bite of the danish and continued, "You said you live in Miami. I've heard so many beautiful things about that city. Many country club members have condominiums there, and they visit the city frequently. The ladies tell me there are gorgeous shops, and many fine restaurants in Miami. What do you there?"

Alma loved to talk to the ladies at the country club. They would always tell her about their travels to Europe and the United States. They traveled frequently to

Miami, since it was the closest American city to Caracas. They usually brought her back souvenirs, and often brought her some clothes. She had seen pictures of Miami, and especially liked how romantic South Beach looked.

"I own a successful car business and I also own many buildings throughout the city and other states. It wasn't easy, and it took many years for me to reach this status. I was born in Miami, but my family is originally from Havana, Cuba. My father had a successful car business there, but when Castro came he lost it all. He moved to Miami to start a new life and with hopes of starting a new business, but it was harder than he thought. He turned to alcohol and the only type of work he found was low paying jobs."

Roberto continued telling her how he remembered his father working at a car wash in the morning, and as a janitor in the evening. The family hardly saw him and when he would come home, they would all be asleep. His mother was used to the good life in Havana. It was extremely hard for her to get used to this new life-style. However, she didn't let this negative event affect her character. She had always been very religious and her strong faith in God kept her happy. She was their constant motivator, and she knew they would succeed. Because of her motivation, his older brother is a doctor in New York, and his younger sister just graduated from Harvard Law School. Roberto took after his father, so when he graduated from college, he started his own business. He learned the tricks of the trade, as they say, and together with a strong will to succeed he became a millionaire by the time he was thirty. He is thirty-six now.

Roberto's story deeply impacted Alma. She saw a man who was determined to accomplish anything. It didn't matter what obstacles were in his way. Roberto felt comfortable speaking to Alma about his family's struggle. He knew she would be able to identify with him.

"Wow, that's an interesting story. I know your mother must be very proud of all of her children. She reminds me of my mother. It seems Hispanic mothers are very protective of their children. I know it's because they love us and want the best for us. But in your case, it paid off handsomely. Pardon the intrusion, but I assume a man of your status must be married by now?" Alma was now intrigued by Roberto, and knowing he was a millionaire made it that more exciting.

"You assume correctly, however, there is no wife at the current time. But I was married for a brief period. My wife died in a car accident. She and a friend were driving back from an afternoon of shopping, when a drunk driver crashed into them. They were both killed on impact. She was pregnant with our first child. I can only think of how our lives would have been. It's been five years since her death. I've been unable to start a relationship with another woman. I can't help compare them to Lorena; that was her name. Ironically, I met her in a restaurant in South Beach. She was visiting from Mexico City, and we gradually fell in love with each other. For a year I would fly there to visit her, and she would fly to Miami to see me."

Roberto continued. "We had a beautiful wedding in San Miguel de Allende, that was her dream. She wanted to have the wedding in that historical Mexican city. It was special to both of us, because we spent many weekends there."

"I am so sorry to hear that. I am crying because I can feel that you loved her dearly. I cannot imagine what it's like to lose the person you love the most so tragically. I myself will be devastated when I lose my own mother. I cannot fathom meeting the man of my dreams, and then losing him in an accident. But you must go on with your life, Roberto. You are still young, and you have a passion for living. But most important, I can see that you would be faithful to your new wife. I can see that you would love her very much. That is, if anyone will ever get the chance to replace Lorena in your heart."

They continued talking, and then Alma looked at her watch and noticed it was almost five thirty.

"Oh, my God I have to get going or I'll miss the next bus. It takes about half an hour to get to my neighborhood. Thank you so much for inviting me, Roberto. I enjoyed your company, and I will ask the *Virgencita* to bring a special woman into your life."

"Alma, wait, you're forgetting the pastries. It will only take a minute to have them placed in a box." Roberto wasn't going to let this moment escape from him. He already felt something special for Alma. He wasn't about to let her take the bus home.

"Alma, have I been able to convince you that I'm trustworthy? You don't have to take the bus. I can get you home faster. Besides, you'll have the chance to ride in a Mercedes Benz."

Alma looked over her shoulders, and noticed that Sara and Raul were nodding in approval. That was a reassuring sign for her, and she gladly accepted Roberto's invitation.

The Mercedes Benz drove up to the old wooden house where Alma lived. Roberto stepped out, went around, and opened the door for Alma. Her hands were sweating, and she felt like a queen riding in that exotic car. Her heart was pounding intensely, and she knew she was starting to fall in love with Roberto. Dolores was outside gardening when she saw the car pull up in front of her house. She was shocked to see Alma coming out of the car. To her knowledge,

Alma had never been in such an expensive car. More importantly, she wanted to know whom this man was that had the audacity to bring her daughter home.

"Mama, how are you doing, I'm so happy to see you. Let me introduce you to Don Roberto Del Mar. He lives in Miami, but his family is originally from Havana, Cuba. I met him at the country club today, and he invited me to Café Paris after work for some cappuccino and pastries. He's returning to Miami tomorrow evening. Oh, here are some pastries for you and Rosa."

Roberto walked towards Dolores and shook her hand. He saw how much Alma resembled her mother. He could picture Dolores looking exactly like Alma when she was younger.

"You have a beautiful daughter, I can see where she gets her beauty from. You are a very beautiful woman as well. Before you get mad at Alma, I'd like to tell you that it was my idea to bring her home. In fact, I insisted on it, since I wanted her to come home on time. I know that you are very protective of her, and I commend you for the excellent manner in which you have raised her. I would like to develop a closer relationship with your family, and I want to help you in any way I can."

"Thank you for being so kind to my daughter, Mr. Del Mar. My name is Dolores Zertuche, *para servirle.* And I appreciate you understanding my strictness with Alma. I don't want her to struggle through life the way that I've had to. She is very smart and I want her to live a life that is pleasing to God and the *Virgencita. Esta es su casa.* You can come here whenever you are in town. Can I get you a glass of water?"

"Oh no thank you. I must be heading back to my hotel since I have a special presentation tonight. I will be in the country club tomorrow again, so I will see you there in the morning Alma.

It was a pleasure meeting you Señora Zertuche, and I look forward to seeing you on my next visit to Caracas. *Hasta Luego y Dios la bendiga."* Roberto got into the car and drove off.

"I hope you're not mad at me for letting Roberto bring me home. He insisted, after I told him I was running late to catch the next bus. And besides, Sara and Raul gave me their approval for going with him. I think I'm falling in love."

"How do you know you're falling in love. You just met him today and only spent an afternoon with him. Love takes time to build, *hija,* it's not that easy. Besides, how do you know that he's not like the other men that just want you for pleasure? No, Alma, we have to get to know him better before I allow you to go further with him. We don't know anything about him." Dolores was obviously upset at Alma's innocent reply.

"But mama, you don't understand. He is different than the rest of those men. He told me his story in the café. It was so romantic being with him. But it was sad at the same time. You see, Roberto is a widow. His wife died in a car accident five years ago. She was pregnant with their first baby. He has not been able to fall in love again. Mama, he is looking for his next wife. I can see he's serious about me. Don't you see, mama, he's the type of man you always wanted me to marry. He is also a millionaire." Alma took the pastry box from her mother and went inside the house.

Dolores suddenly changed her attitude. This man was a widow and a millionaire. Maybe the *Virgencita* had finally answered her prayers. Roberto, was in fact, the type of man that she had wanted for Alma. Although, he wasn't perfectly handsome, he was courteous and well educated. "*Ay, Virgencita ayudame.* Give me a sign that Roberto is the right man for my daughter. You know I want her to be happy. I love her so much and I don't want her to suffer like I have. Oh God, this poor woman is begging for mercy. Please help us make the right decision." Dolores made the sign of the cross upon herself.

◆　　◆　　◆

The next day Alma got up early to head for the country club. She wanted to see Roberto so badly, and she knew he would be having breakfast there. When she arrived, she was looking around the breakfast room to see if she could find him. A sizable crowd had already gathered, and she went from table to table trying to find Roberto. But there was no sign of him. She headed back to the kitchen area, when all of sudden she felt someone tap her on the shoulder. "Looking for me?" Roberto surprised her, and at once she could feel her heart pound intensely. "Why no, I was just checking to see who needed to be served. How are you this morning, Roberto?"

"I am doing just great. I slept well last night. After my presentation I was feeling tired, and I think that helped. But most important of all, I wanted to get a good night sleep so I could feel better today. I didn't want you to see me with a tired look on my face."

"Oh, Roberto you're so funny. You always look good. You even look ten years younger than your age. I like the Polo shirt you're wearing today, and what is that cologne you have on?" Alma loved to see men dressed elegantly.

"It's called Guerlain, it's a fragrance that has been around for years. It was my father's favorite cologne, when times were better for him. Now it's my favorite. Do you like the fragrance?"

"It's different. It has a distinguishing scent, and it goes well with you. And, yes I like it a lot." Alma's smile sent chills through Roberto's body.

Roberto sat down to have breakfast, and then chatted with a few of the club's members. He lit up another Cuban cigar. He could not take his eyes away from Alma, as she strolled up and down the room.

Roberto played a full game of golf that morning, and then went back to look for Alma. She was getting ready to leave for the day and he offered to take her home again. She accepted once again. They got in the car and drove off.

"Alma, there is something I have to tell you. I have only known you for two days now, but I'm captivated by you. You are a very special lady and meeting you has changed my outlook on life. I thought I would never be able to find love again, but you have changed that. You have that wholesome personality that is so hard to find in today's society. You have many of Lorena's characteristics, although you are unique in your own way. I want you to understand that I have not quite gotten over her. But if I'm to fall in love again, I want it to be with someone like you. I know you can help me with the personal struggles I am going through. I know I will love you dearly, and I will be faithful to you. Will you give me the opportunity to develop a relationship with you? I will make you the queen of my life, and I will build a castle for you. I will make you the happiest woman alive, and make all of your dreams come true."

"Roberto, that is so nice. I've never been proposed to like this before. I mean, I've had other type of proposals, but never one like this. I don't know what to say. I'd like to get to know you better before I make such a decision. I really don't know much about you, and you don't know much about me. And you have to get to know my mother and my sister better too. And I have to get to know your father and mother as well. I can't just make a decision so quickly. I hope you understand."

Deep inside Alma wanted to say a rousing "yes". She wanted to accept his proposal and start a relationship with him.

She dreamed about moving to Miami and starting a new life. She imagined living in a big house, and having money to buy clothes. She would finally travel around the world. But she couldn't let him see her true feelings. She had to show him that she was not desperate to get married.

Roberto knew that Alma liked him too. And he also knew that she was being proper, and was not going to show her true feelings. He knew men would kill to be able to marry a woman like her. Convincing her mother to allow him to marry her would be easy. Money was the answer. Once Dolores knew that Alma would be living in high society, she would give him instant approval. Besides, he would support Dolores and Rosa in Caracas and improve their standard of living.

Roberto went inside the house and spoke to Dolores about his intentions with Alma. He told her he wanted permission to court Alma and eventually marry her. Dolores cried and gave him the approval and then turned to Alma to hug her. He knew Roberto's intentions were honest, and this was the man for her daughter. She looked up and gave thanks to God and the *Virgencita*.

Their courtship continued for the next few months. Roberto was fully convinced that he wanted to marry Alma.

Roberto told them the wedding would be in Caracas, so that all of their friends and family could attend. It would be held at the country club, since that is where they met. He would take care of all the wedding arrangements. He sent Alma to an upscale wedding shop, so she could buy the gown of her choice.

He also paid for Dolores and Rosa's dresses, and all of the bridesmaids. He wanted this to be Caracas's most elaborate wedding. It would be held in two months.

He told them he would start providing for the family immediately, and he set up a bank account in Dolores's name, and he also bought them a new car. He owned several houses in Caracas, so he had the family move to a better neighborhood. This was all a dream come true for Alma and her mother.

The wedding day came, and the ceremony was held outside in a gazebo. Alma looked stunning, and she had the appearance of a Caracas socialite. Rosa was her maid of honor. Many of Alma's friends and family were there and they were happy at how lucky she was. They knew she would have a completely different life in the United States. Knowing she was marrying a millionaire would change her life forever. "Don't' forget about us poor folks here in Caracas, Alma," said a little old lady who had known Alma all of her life. "Oh, don't say that Olivia, you know I will always be a part of you. I can never, ever forget you. I consider you all my family. Thank you, for coming."

Roberto and Alma finally left for their honeymoon in the Fiji Islands, and spent one week there. For the first time Alma experienced the pleasures of being with a man. Roberto knew she was inexperienced, and he made this moment special for Alma. It was also special for him. Since Lorena's death, he had not slept with a woman he loved. They made love many times throughout the week, and she enjoyed this new sensation. They strolled together along the beach, and the island's beauty was fascinating. It was heaven on earth indeed for Alma.

They traveled for the next three weeks to Europe. They visited Rome, Venice, Madrid, and of course Paris. Alma finally got her chance to travel around the world. She went shopping everywhere, and on the way back they stopped in New York City.

There she walked through and shopped the stores on Fifth Avenue, Madison Avenue, and Broadway. She went to Bloomingdale's, Lord and Taylor, Macy's, Saks Fifth Avenue, and her favorite, Tiffany's. Roberto bought her an expensive diamond necklace there. She was now a woman of distinction, and she came to Miami with a different attitude towards life.

The years went by and Alma gave birth to two beautiful children, Roberto, Jr. and Alyssa. Her mother and sister now live in Miami too. Rosa married a professional baseball player that she met at one of Alma's social parties.

Alma loves Roberto for having changed her life and for telling her daily how much he loves her.

I Love To Be Loved By You

As the sun rises in the morning,
and I realize it's another day,
I gently open my eyes hoping
to see you, and hear "I love you"
as you so adoringly say.

You are my reason for living,
my one and only desire.
How I long for your touch,
for it lifts me so higher.
The warmth of your body
makes me want you so much.
And when you finally kiss me,
I ask, "Is there a better love than such?"

I love you so much,
and I thank life for you.
You have loved me so dearly
and I don't know why.
But I can see it so clearly,
you will love me until the day that I die.

A Love That Lasts Forever

I have loved you all my life,
for you have been there for me.
In my times of joy and in my times of sorrow
you stood by me and loved me profoundly.

I don't understand how you could love me so,
knowing how imperfect I am always.
I've let you down so many, many times,
yet you were still there during those difficult days.

My life would mean nothing without you.
I live everyday only for you.
Your love is far greater than I ever imagined.
So many times I wanted to give up,
only to feel your love lifting my spirits,
as you softly said, "I will love you forever".

I Love The Way You Look At Me

When you look at me I melt.
You don't know how good it makes me feel,
when I see your eyes staring at mine.
My whole body is wired with a heavenly sensation.

Valentine's Day—A Day For Love

How truly beautiful it is to love someone.
How truly blessed it feels to be loved by someone.
Love is the most wonderful feeling we can experience in this life.
Love is shared by two people who need to be together.
Love is also shared with others who have brought joy into our lives.
But love is also shared within ourselves.
We have to love who we are before we can show love to others.
On this special day let us share love with those close to us.
And let's also share it with others.
Love is not just romantic love.
Love is not just passion.
Love is giving of oneself.
For true love only comes from God, who will love us forever.
While we're still here on earth, He wants us to show true love to others.
Give someone a kiss, give someone a hug.
Tell someone you love them, tell someone else you appreciate them.
Give someone some flowers, give someone else some chocolates.
Make this day a special day of Love.
Make this day a special day for the whole world.
Give this world your Love.

May you have a Loving Valentine's Day

OUR FOODS

Family Barbecue

Perhaps, the unofficial event that brings most Hispanic families together is the family barbecue. Not a weekend goes by where a barbecue isn't being cooked up in somebody's backyard.

Chicken, beef, hamburgers, hot dogs, *chorizo* (sausage), ribs, and brisket all smell and taste so good when cooked on a barbecue grill. Together with your choice of the following: potato salad, beans, *tortillas,* bread, *jalapeños,* corn, green beans, *congris* (rice and beans), *arroz con gandules* (rice with pigeon peas) and a great salad. And, of course: plenty of drinks for everyone to enjoy.

To finish it all up, what better way than with a succulent dessert. Apple pie, peach cobbler, pecan pie, guava pastries, *flan, tres leches* cake, or a chocolate cake.

Then everyone gathers around to talk about the good times, and about how well life is treating all of them. The mothers brag about their children, the fathers brag or nag about their jobs, the children talk among themselves, and then everyone shares some gossip.

There may be some misunderstandings, and people may get upset at each other. Family gatherings, unfortunately, can turn into griping sessions too.

But funny how we all can come together on the next barbecue, and start all over again.

My Passion for Cuban Food

An invitation to have dinner at a Cuban friend's home is like being invited to dine in the White House. Especially when I know that the lady of the house is an excellent cook. As soon as I enter the house I am entranced by the smell of the rich Cuban cooking. I am given a warm welcome and told to come inside.

I anxiously wait in the family room, chatting and watching movies on the DVD player with my friend. We talk about life in Cuba, and whether we will ever see it free again. Then, we share our dreams about "making it in America". He wants to start a jewelry store, and has big plans for the future. He and his wife have only been in America for eight years, and they already own a home and two cars. They have learned to save their money and spend it wisely. I admire their wisdom and their drive to succeed. I tell him about my next venture in becoming an author. He had already seen me in my previous attempt to succeed with my gourmet coffee shop. He, in turn, admires me for my optimism, and for not letting a business failure set me back.

His wife finally tells us that the food is ready. We sit at the table, and the other guests who were invited finally arrive. She has set the table and everything looks and smells terrific.

The main course consists of Cuban style breaded steak, black beans and white rice, *tostones* (fried green plantains), a salad, Cuban bread, and the Cuban soda *Materva,* although there are other traditional American sodas.

As I start tasting the food it takes me back to childhood, and I remember my special times with my parents. This was the food I grew up with, and unbeknownst to many, my father was the official cook of the family.

The breaded steak is simply out of this world, and so are the beans and rice. I feel like a king eating that food. I also can't help thinking of all the Cubans in Cuba, who would want to eat as richly as I am. I know someday that will eventually happen. But for now I thank God for bringing me to America.

After we finish the meal, his wife brings out a beautiful *flan.* I learned to eat this custard type dessert in Miami. There are many variations, and I have become a flan connoisseur, so to speak. When I taste one, I know how good it really is. This one was simply fabulous. Cubans eat a lot of sweets, and we have special tastes for desserts. It's part of our culture. One that I'm thankful for, since I love sweets.

But, that's not the end of the meal. It wouldn't be a Cuban dinner without a cup of Cuban coffee. I can smell the coffee brewing in the kitchen. When she finally brings it to me, and I take a sip, it adds the finishing touch to a wonderful meal.

I Love Mexican Food

We enter the restaurant, and the aroma of the delicious food quickly permeates through our respiratory system. Suddenly, we feel hungrier than we were a few minutes ago.

The hostess helps us find a seat, and hands us the menu. The waiter brings complimentary nacho chips with the house salsa.

The mariachi band starts playing beautiful love ballads, which fill the place with a sense of romanticism.

We settle on ordering a traditional Mexican plate. It includes a crispy taco, two cheese enchiladas, a *chalupa,* together with refried beans and rice. We can't wait!

The order finally arrives, and first the waiter sets down a porcelain container, that holds freshly made warm flour tortillas. Then, he places our plates in front of us, and warns us that they are extremely hot. He also tells us the story behind the special salsa. He asks if we need anything else before he leaves, and we tell him everything looks good.

We each take out a warm tortilla, and fold it, as we were taught in childhood. Then, we begin tasting the food, and how really good it tastes. We pour some of the hot salsa on top of the enchiladas and tacos, and the taste is out of this world. Then, we taste the refried beans and the rice, and they are so heavenly delicious. I love onions with my enchiladas, something the chef must have known.

The finale is when we order some *empanadas* and hot Mexican style chocolate. *Delicioso!*

The Diversity in Hispanic Breakfasts

Having been raised in two Hispanic cultures, I can appreciate the different types of foods. In Texas, the breakfast taco has become an icon, and is now an official Texas breakfast. Both Hispanics and non-Hispanics have become accustomed to starting their day with one of these delicious concoctions. A breakfast taco consists of flour or corn tortilla, filled with your choice of eggs, bacon, potatoes, sausage, *chorizo,* beans, *fajita*; *carne guisada*; or the famous *barbacoa* tacos. The other popular breakfast plate in Texas consists of *huevos rancheros* (ranch style eggs). These are cooked over easy and placed on top of a fried corn tortilla, served with refried beans, and hot salsa, and accompanied by flour tortillas.

The Cuban breakfast is not as spectacular, but it's also delicious. I learned to eat the different types of Cuban breakfasts during my seven years in Miami. The most common is the *café con leche* with *Cuban tostadas* (Cuban bread toast). These tostadas are delicious with butter, and taste so good with a sweetened *café con leche.* The other traditional breakfast is simply ham, eggs, and Cuban toast. You can also have a Spaniard tortilla (egg omelet), that is made with Spanish sausage, or with ham.

Once a Panamanian friend, whose mother is from El Salvador, invited me to have breakfast at a Salvadoran restaurant. She introduced me to this type of food, which I found to be simply appetizing. It consisted of *pupusas (a tiny round and filling tortilla)* that is very common in Central American countries. The breakfast is served with eggs, and the *pupusas* are served with a special cheese made of goat milk. It had a very interesting taste that added a special touch to the discovery of this new type of food for me. It is one of my more memorable breakfasts, since the restaurant was small and the service was excellent.

Nothing Beats a Spanish Paella

The grand dame of the Hispanic foods has got to be the Spanish paella. This delicious rice dish is one of the gifts that our Spanish ancestors gave us. There are many different ways to make paella. But whatever the ingredients, it's the overall taste that will make it distinguished. It normally consists of rice, and different types of seafood mixed together. It has a wonderful taste that makes me wish I lived in Spain.

I remember the first time I had the honor of tasting this dish. It was with a group of friends, and we were having a good time. They also ordered some sangria to go with it. I had never had this drink before, and I enjoyed the taste.

It turned out to be a terrific evening for all of us. I was just wondering why I hadn't been introduced to paella before.

I'm dying to have some right now as I write this.

Ole!

Cuban Coffee

I unscrew the Italian espresso maker, and I wash it thoroughly.
I pour in some water, and I place some ground espresso in the container.
I use either Pilon or Bustelo coffee, for an authentic Cuban taste.
I screw the whole thing back up tightly.
And I place it on top of the stove.
I turn on the stove, and set it on high.
Within two minutes, the coffee starts to brew.
Immediately, the aroma of freshly brewed coffee fills the whole house.
I pour the coffee on a miniature espresso cup.
And then I put a hefty amount of sugar.
Azuca!
Once again I'm ready to enjoy this mystical brew.

PERSONAL TREASURES

The Class of '78

It was around March 1998, when I realized that it had almost been twenty years since I had graduated from high school. I remember the exact date of that historic day: **May 25, 1978**.

This day was destined to be the last time that I would see most of the classmates that I had attended school for five years. Deep down inside, none of us really wanted this moment to come. It was something we had been working towards all of our young lives, because it meant we had accomplished something incredible. It was something that for many in previous generations only signified a dream. But we really didn't want it all to end so soon.

Now, here we were walking towards the stage to receive our diplomas. What I remember most distinctly was how disorganized the ceremony turned out to be. The master of ceremony, a popular school counselor, was so nervous that he just kept reading the names of the graduates without looking up to see if the right graduate was standing there. Once we got on stage our names had already been read way before we got our diploma. That wasn't the way it was supposed to have been. It was supposed to have been a more structured evening full of wonderful memories.

We were the mighty Class of '78 of J.W. Nixon High School in Laredo, Texas. No other class in our school's recent history had had as many talented and distinguished students. Many local prominent families were gathered there that evening since their children were also graduating. I was privileged to have belonged to this exceptional group of students. It was the next best thing to having attended a private school.

I, for one, was glad this chapter of my life was over because I had so many things I wanted to accomplish. Throughout high school I knew that I was talented, but I felt I hadn't been given the opportunity to exhibit these to their full potential. I partly blamed my frustration with who I was as the basis for this feeling. Very few of my classmates knew what my background was. They probably figured my family was originally from Laredo, or that we had moved from another place in the state of Texas. It's funny how I knew so much about them, but they knew very little about me.

I embraced their Mexican-American culture: their speaking habits, their food, their traditions, their fears, their hopes, their dreams. But few of them knew that I was an immigrant from Cuba, whose traditions and culture were totally different than theirs. In America I was now a Hispanic, living in another Hispanic culture, and feeling lost and confused. I was Cuban on the inside, but Hispanic on the outside. My family always kept our Cuban traditions alive at home. I would only understand this many years later as a grown adult.

It was in my first year at Lamar Junior High School when I first encountered my new classmates, who would leave me with these memories. I had never seen such beautiful girls before. I remember when I first saw the pretty cheerleaders, I felt so intimidated by their beauty. There was Angie (the most popular), Rosa (the most beautiful), Marta, Elsa, Kathy and Marty. I fell in love with all of them, but unfortunately they didn't feel the same about me. I dreamed about being with them. Even when we reached high school, and many of them had changed, I was still infatuated with them.

Most of them were the daughters of local prominent families, and their mannerisms were very different than the girls I had met in elementary. These girls looked and acted decent, not like the mostly uncultured girls I had gone to elementary school the previous two years. It was a culture shock and a lesson in life for me. I was originally part of the class of '79, but during the summer after seventh grade I enrolled in eighth grade and passed. You see when I moved from Cuba, I was set back one year, since I didn't know English. But I proved to be an excellent student once I learned English. I thoroughly enjoyed my only year at Lamar since I got to see a different perspective in life. It was the beginning of my pursuit of becoming well-cultured myself.

Nixon High School was relatively a new school back in our time and it was almost entirely Hispanic. But it was the school known for its middle-class status, where several students lived in nice homes and vacationed in Europe in the summer. Unfortunately, I didn't belong to that circle, but I dreamed that I would live an extravagant lifestyle as well someday.

Our lives had taken a different turn at Nixon, and it felt strange to see the radical change that many of us went through in high school. Angie continued being the most popular girl in our class for the first two years in high school. There was a new set of cheerleaders (Linda, Mary Margaret), and new popular guys and girls. Those that were once popular in our earlier years eventually lost their status.

I fell in love with other girls who were juniors and seniors, but my introverted personality didn't allow me to pursue them.

Our senior year turned out to be a huge disappointment. The football team lost to our rival high school, and we were all bummed out. It felt weird. We were always used to winning as a class, and we couldn't accept being losers. In all of our years at Nixon we never won the big football game against our rival Martin. But we all felt that it would change in our senior year. Now that I look back, how silly it all really was. Many Martin students attended my father's church, and I came to appreciate them and their school. I think I probably would have been more popular if I would have gone there. At church we would always talk about our school activities, and I would know what was going on over there as well. We also had a few United High students, Laredo's other newest school.

Nevertheless, our basketball team saved the year by winning the district championship. Something the school hadn't experienced before. Finally, we were winners. We knew we were. A new spirit of achievement overtook us all, and now we understood why our class was so great. Funny how sports has a big influence on our school years.

Then came the *60 Minutes* story. I believe it was Mike Wallace who traveled to Laredo to cover the story. The story was about how a poor town like Laredo held an extravagant George Washington Birthday celebration, featuring a mostly Hispanic cast of characters. In other words, how it was the way the local rich families exposed their wealth and status to its poor citizens. Laredo has always been one of the poorest cities in the country. Yet, it has a significant amount of wealthy Hispanics.

One of the highlights of the event is the night when George and Martha Washington present the debutantes into society. Different wealthy men and women represent George and Martha each year, whether Anglo or Hispanic. Traditionally the debutantes are the daughters of the members of the Martha Washington society, and are in their senior year in high school. Most of the debutantes that year were from my graduating class at Nixon High School, thirteen to be precise. There was Rosa, Leticia, Nora, Roberta, Nina, Lamar, Nelda, Celeste, Letti, Emilie, Margaret, Shawn, and Melissa, who was voted as one of the most beautiful girls of our class, and was featured prominently in the story while she took her bow.

I never had the privilege to attend any of these functions, but I was left intrigued by it all. How did these people have the good fortune to be born into this lifestyle? How come I couldn't have experienced all of these events in my life? It was a great make-believe world that had been established for the local rich and continues until this day. But what it did was give me the drive to believe in myself, since most of these people were Hispanic. It made me proud of my Hispanic heritage, and the fact that there are many Hispanics who are refined and well educated. A different perspective than what the media portrays.

In 1988, I was living in Miami when the ten-year class reunion was held. There was no way I could have attended that event, since I was low on funds and very far away. Besides, I was having too much fun meeting new people who admired me, and I didn't want to go back to a time when I felt unappreciated.

Family circumstances brought me back to Texas in 1991. Seven years later many events had taken place: my father's death, my new job as a supervisor, $40,000.00 in my savings account, a new import car, a down payment for a new house, and a new me.

When 1998 began, I didn't know how to get in touch with anyone to find out about our class reunion. I didn't know if I was ready to be reunited with my former classmates, whom I had not heard from for all of these years. But curiosity motivated me to attend this reunion. I contacted the local newspaper, and they gave me the name and telephone number of the person in charge of organizing the event.

I wanted to see how successful these people had become. I wanted to know how life had changed them, and if the pretty girls were still attractive.

Our reunion took place on Labor Day 1998. I was now living in San Antonio, so the trip was only two hours long. My grandmother was still living in Laredo, and I took my mother and my brother on the trip so they could visit her.

I only attended the first night of the reunion, since I had other plans that weekend. It was held in the home of one of the graduates, whose family is exceptionally prominent and well known. The house was located in the city's most prestigious neighborhood, and I had no trouble finding it. The minute I walked into the backyard, where the festivities were taking place, I instantly recognized some faces. I have very good memory, and I remembered many of their names.

More people started coming in and I recognized most of them. Many looked exactly the same, however others were beyond recognition. I was sad and shocked when I heard that some of my classmates had died, due to various circumstances. And yes, many of the pretty girls were still very pretty, and it seemed like I was in my ten-year reunion and not my twenty. Angie was still stunning, and her beauty overtook all of the other women there; Melissa was also still beautiful and showing off her engagement ring, since soon she would be marrying a doctor. Leti remembered my name and we briefly talked about our lives (she also lived in San Antonio and had been voted the class's most popular girl). As Sarita came in I gave her a hug, and told her how I read about her management success in a San Antonio newspaper. I saw Lilly, my former neighbor who didn't recognize me at first since I had changed (for the better) through the years.

I saw Celia who gave me the saddest news of the evening—Ana, one of our classmates had died years before, due to breast cancer. I talked with Rene, who I had met in band, and now works in a prominent San Antonio company, and he was there with his wife, his high school sweetheart. I talked with Mary Margaret, who was a cheerleader, and was now the mother of five children. I saw and met another Leti, who now lived in New Orleans and was expecting a baby. I spoke with San Juanita (who now lived in Dallas); Cindy (another cheerleader) who still looked great; Blanca (who I met in elementary school) and her husband Ray; Maria Elena (the homecoming queen); Dora (the hostess); Jo Emma who took her beautiful teenage daughter; Felipe (the basketball star); Memo (the class president), and many others. I talked all night, and I didn't have anything to eat. I didn't see our class valedictorian Elsa (who I heard was now a doctor), or Linda (our head cheerleader), or Kenny (the football star), or Jose (the other Cuban in school). They may have shown up on either Saturday or Sunday night.

The years had changed all of us, and I had become an extrovert. I talked with so many different people that night, and believe it or not, I met some of them for the very first time. I never had the opportunity to talk to them in high school, and it was interesting to find out what their lives had become since then.

Several of my classmates were now attorneys, doctors, teachers, school counselors, school principals, accountants, entrepreneurs, managers, dentists, pharmacists, college professors, and housewives too. Some of them had gone through divorces, and many of them were already parents of teenage children. Many had moved away to other cities within Texas and throughout the nation. But this event brought us all back. I found out that, like me, many had not attended the ten-year reunion, and somehow they felt compelled to attend this reunion.

But, what I remember most from that evening was seeing how these people had had an incredible impact in my life. I was so happy that many of them had turned out so successful in their professions and their lives. At the same time, I was proud to see that this mostly Hispanic group of people were living the American dream. Unbeknownst to them, they probably didn't realize that this was what their parents or grandparents had come to this country for. They had wanted their descendants to have a better life than theirs.

Twenty years had changed our lives, but our dreams still kept us reaching for the stars. I will always remember my former classmates, and the happy moments they gave me. I refuse to think about the negative events, for they are long gone and forgotten. We are all different people today, much older, but so much wiser.

We will always be the class of '78!

Andy's Christmas Wish

Andy was walking downtown Havana with his mother.
This was Cuba in the late 1960's.
All of sudden they stopped at a toy store, and his eyes looked intensely at the display window.
He was admiring the big red toy car that was right in the middle of the window.
Andy looked up and said to his mother,
"Mommy, I want that big red car for Christmas."
His mother looked at him almost crying
and she said, "We don't have enough money to buy it, Andy."
She looked up to the sky as if pleading with God.
"I know we'll get the money somehow mommy," said Andy with a huge smile.
The mother smiled back and gave him a hug.
As they were walking away from the toy store,
Andy couldn't help but look back at his favorite toy.

The family was going through tough times since
they lived in a poor third world country where communism ruled.
Every day the father would check the mail waiting for
that important document that would give them permission to leave the country.
The family would gather daily to have dinner together.
Food was beginning to get scarce, but somehow there
was always enough for the whole family to share.
They would begin the meal with a prayer, and many
times other neighborhood kids would join them,
since their families didn't have enough food left to feed them.

It was that country's tradition to celebrate Three Kings Day
every January sixth, and Andy knew that the kings would certainly grant him his wish.
He saw his parents leave the day before, and asked them where they were going,
"To visit the kings," his father responded. "We have a long journey, but we'll be

back soon."
He was so excited, and he knew he would get his favorite toy.
He ran back inside the house and headed to see grandma.
"Grandma, mommy and daddy are going to see the three kings."
He wrapped his arms around her, and she was filled with emotion.
His sister saw what was happening and she jealously said,
"Well, they are going to bring me gifts too."
He walked towards her and hugged her also and said,
"I know they are sister, cause I've been praying for your presents too."

It was night when the parents got back, and Andy could see the tired look on their faces.
"Did you see them mommy, did you tell them what I wanted?"
"Did you also tell them what sister wanted, did you?"
The father sat down on the sofa and nodded, as to say they did.
The mother told him there was a long line of people waiting to
speak with the three kings, but they finally saw them.

The three kings told them they had many requests for toys.
They weren't sure if they would be able to grant their wish.
But nevertheless, the mother told Andy that the kings would be by tonight, while he was sleeping.
But first, he needed to leave a bowl full of water on the porch,
so that the kings' camels would be able to drink from it.

With the help of his grandma, Andy took a bowl
and filled it with water and placed it outside on the porch.
Andy and his older sister went to bed early that night.
He was hoping he would get his favorite toy and his sister was hoping for hers too.
The parents and grandma stayed up talking about their day's ordeal.
They couldn't find the children's toys, since there were barely any left.
There were long lines everywhere they went, since communism
had robbed the country of the rich capitalism it once was known for.
They were just hoping that the children would be happy with their toys.

The next day Andy woke up early, once he saw that it was daylight.
He sneaked carefully out of his room, and went to go look in the living room.
He saw there were several presents wrapped up by the Christmas tree,

and he wondered which ones were his.
He knew the three kings had been there the night before.
He opened the locked front door, and he saw that the water was all gone.
He could only imagine what the three kings and the camels looked like.

The time finally arrived when the family gathered at the tree,
and presents were handed out. Andy was all smiles.
First, they gave his sister her present and when she opened it,
it was a beautiful doll, with red cheeks and golden hair.
She was so happy she knew she would be the envy of the neighborhood girls.
Next, it was Andy's turn, and when he opened his present it wasn't
what he was hoping for, it was a toy train. His parents could
immediately see the disappointed look on his face.

His mother reached over to him and told him the three kings
were very sorry, but they ran out of the big toy car he was hoping for.
"Honey," said Andy's mother "they promised you would receive it next year."
They want you to have this train so you can transport all those people
who can't afford to buy a car. Please understand that they really love you and
so do we." Andy looked at his mother and gave her a hug and said
"I know mommy, I love you too. I know that when we get to America I'll
get my big toy car, and have many other toys, too."

Andy took the toy train and started playing with it.
He played with it all day long, until the train wouldn't function anymore.
"Look mommy, the train doesn't work anymore." With that he fell asleep.
The parents and grandma looked at each other, and laughed since
they knew the toy was of poor quality. The toys were being imported from
another communist country.

The year went by and the country's economic situation continued to deteriorate.
One day Andy told his mother "Mommy, we are going to receive the
telegram today telling us that we can leave the country. We are finally going to
the
United States, and I will have all the toys in the world."
The mother didn't pay much attention to him, and found it peculiar that
her son would be so perceptive. Unbeknownst to her, Andy had
been listening to their conversations, and he knew that they needed to
receive a document giving them permission to leave the country.

Around noon, someone was knocking on the door, and Andy's
father answered it. The man at the door handed him a package, and asked him to
sign a paper.
The whole family was gathered at the living room, and the father opened the
package.
He opened it, and read the letter, and started jumping up and down for joy.
They had been granted permission to leave the country for America.
The little boy's mother was startled, for she could not believe what was happening.
How did her son know that this document was coming today? Did he have
some sort of special psychic powers? How could he have been so sure?

It took the family several months before they could leave the country.
But finally, the day arrived for their departure to America.
The country's authorities gave them a hard time at the airport.
Many families who had also received their permission to leave
were gathered at the airport. The look of worry and anticipation was on every-
one's
faces, since they didn't know what the future held for them in America.
Many had lost their entire property and wealth to the new regime.
They didn't know how they were going to survive in their new country.
The trip was relatively short, and they finally arrived on American soil in Miami.
A group of American missionaries was waiting for Andy's family at the airport.
Andy was astounded as to how tall the Americans were. He had never seen
so many people with blonde hair and blue eyes before. They were talking
to him, but he could not understand what they were telling him. One of the men
reached over and patted him on the head. Another lady grabbed his cheeks,
and told him how cute he was. But he didn't know what she had just told him.

Andy's family arrived a week before Christmas, and were placed
in a home utilized to house other people from the same country.
Andy was the center of attention, always roaming around the house
getting to know other kids. They had a teacher who was teaching them
English, and he was enjoying learning this new language.
The teacher told them that in this country the three kings
didn't bring children toys. But not to worry, because they had
designated a man named Santa Claus to give toys in America.
She reminded them that on Christmas Day, Santa was going to

pay them a special visit, and would grant them their wish.
Andy was certain that he would get his big red toy car.

When Christmas Day finally arrived the teacher took the kids
into a room. When she opened the door there was Santa Claus, sitting in the
middle of the room. Andy couldn't believe his eyes. The room was full of toys!
The teacher told them "Santa said to pick whatever toy you want, and its yours."
Andy rushed in and he looked all over the place. Then all of a sudden his eyes
looked over to the corner of the room, and there it was.
A big red toy car. The one he had wished for last year in his native country.

He ran over to it, and he saw two other boys running towards it too.
But he beat them to it, and sat right in. It was his to keep. He was so happy.
He saw his sister with a beautiful doll in her hands.
And then he noticed his parents and his grandma, and he waved at them.
They came over to see him and he told his mother,
"See mommy, I told you I would get my big red toy car. This is the
best present I have ever gotten in my life!

Tears were building inside his parents eyes. They had sacrificed everything to
come to America, so that their children would have a better life.

As the years went by, Andy became a man.
He graduated from high school, then went to college, and became a successful
businessman.
He always remembers that special Christmas, and he has not experienced one like
that again.

He now gives back to others the kind of love he was shown when
he was that little boy, who had big dreams and aspirations.
And he is thankful that he lives in America, the best country in the world.

He now drives a real red sports car.
His Christmas wish really came true.

If I Were a Millionaire

How I wish that I could have a million dollars,
then all my troubles would go away.
I wouldn't have to worry about getting up
everyday to go to work.
I wouldn't have to worry about getting my boss's approval.
I would stay home and do lots of reading.
I would travel around the world.
I would live in a mansion and have a personal chef.
I would shop at all the exclusive places.
I would have a collection of expensive cars.
I would have the most beautiful wife in the world.
I would play golf and tennis every day.
I wouldn't have to worry about not having enough money.
I would attend many sporting events.
I would go to every concert and Broadway production.
I would meet the President of the United States.
I would own the best stereo system.
I would have a personal trainer and a gym.
I would be very influential in my city.
I would write a book on how I acquired my wealth.
I would buy my sister and her husband a house.
I would help my brother start a business and buy him a new truck.
I would give a substantial amount of money to my closest friends.
I would give more money to the church and other charities.
I would sponsor poor children in this country to give them a better life.
I would invest a great portion of my money to secure my future.
I would have many new friends and long lost relatives that I didn't know existed.
I would have many people envious and jealous of me.
If I had a million dollars, I would probably have no peace of mind.

A Rich and Snobbish Hispanic

I have been accused of being many things.
It depends in which social circle we've had the honor of meeting.
But one thing is certain, I have always enjoyed the finer things in life.
Call me a snob. Go ahead, accuse me of being arrogant.
It doesn't really matter to me, because you're probably right.
I see nothing wrong with wanting to live in an upscale neighborhood,
and having a mansion for a house, on top of a hill.
I love expensive exotic cars, especially those that attract attention.
But don't they all attract attention?
I love Mercedes Benz, BMW, Porsche, Ferrari and Rolls Royce,
why not?
I love to vacation in Europe, the Fiji Islands, Monte Carlo, and the South of
France.
I love to shop at Macy's, and Saks in New York, at the shops along Beverly Hill's
Rodeo Drive, and Chicago's Michigan Avenue.
I always have to have the latest in fashion.
I eat at expensive restaurants, and relax at the country club.
I love to play golf, work out at a trendy gym, and play tennis.
I love to go to a spa and have a relaxing massage.
I love to mingle with successful and wealthy people.
I love to attend charity functions and flash my wealth.
But more than anything else, I love having the money
to be able to do all of these things.

**This is dedicated to all those Hispanics who have achieved the coveted
status of being wealthy. (And every day this number increases.) Enjoy
your success, and don't feel ashamed about it.
You are our inspiration.
I hope to join this exclusive group one day too.**

A Tribute To Our Hispanic Soldiers

Our nation changed dramatically after the acts of terrorism that occurred on September 11, 2001. We were all shocked by these senseless acts and we felt highly offended by those that were behind these attacks.

I remember, when I visited New York for the first time in September 1996, and I took pictures from the top of the World Trade Center. I also visited Ellis Island, and I saw the special exhibit they had as a tribute to all of the immigrants that came to this nation. Then I went to the Statue of Liberty, and what a beautiful sight that was. Earlier in the week I had been in Washington D.C., and I visited the White House, the Capitol, the Smithsonian Institution, and the Lincoln Memorial. How proud I felt to be an American. How proud I felt at being raised in this great country.

The night when President Bush declared war on Iraq, I sat down and wrote the following article for a Christian online magazine where I was a regular columnist:

God Offers Us His Peace During Times of War

As I sit down to write this article, it's been about thirty minutes since the United States began its attack on Iraq. The President spoke earlier tonight to inform the nation that the war was officially starting. Saddam Hussein failed to leave Iraq within the specified time that the United States had given him. Our nation had no other alternative but to proceed with war. Almost all of the television and radio stations preempted their regular programming to focus on the coverage of the war. Today, March 19, 2003, marks another date in our nation's history as we once again go to war to fight for our freedom. It was twelve years ago that we were involved in another war—The Gulf War. That war was no comparison to the Vietnam War, which caused much devastation—both physical and well as emotional, because of its length. We don't know yet the ramifications that this new war will bestow on us. But regardless of the impact that it leaves, war is always something we want to avoid.

For most children in America this is the first time that they are experiencing a war. Many of these children's parents are somehow involved in the war. Here in San Antonio we have many military families who are in one way or another being impacted by this war. Our city also feels compassion for all of these soldiers and their families due to our history as a military city. When they are happy, we are happy. But when they are sad, we share in their sorrow.

Americans of all ages and races are now united as one to defend our country. We want to maintain the peace that our forefathers fought so intensely to make this the best country in the world. But there are evil forces around the world that want to stop us from enjoying this freedom. Unfortunately, war is the only answer when our nation is threatened so severely.

War's most negative effect has to be the loss of lives—both innocent lives as well as lives of those like Hussein who are the main targets. White House spokesman Ari Fleischer said tonight "Americans ought to be prepared for loss of life." This means that it is expected that some American soldiers will die in this war. Many of these soldiers will never see their wives and children again. It will not be until these children are grown adults that they will fully understand why their fathers sacrificed their lives.

How do we Christians react to war in this time and age? The Bible is full of war stories, but somehow we don't like to connect our modern world to that period. We feel that we have surpassed those barbaric customs and we shouldn't have to resort to war in this era. But what hasn't changed is the human heart. War usually starts inside of us and then it escalates to the level of confrontation. We all go through different types of war daily—whether it's at home, the work place, at church, or within ourselves. Disagreements, jealousy, envy, the need to control others—these all lead to war on a personal level, as well as on an international level.

We Christians need to take this time of world war to pray to God, through His Son Jesus Christ. We need to pray for our Nation, our President, our Cabinet, our Soldiers and their Families, our Allies, all Americans, for Peace, and we need to pray for all the people of the world. We need to set the example to all of those that don't share our faith, and we need to show them that we have a God who is solemn and is with us in every circumstance. This is one of the best opportunities to witness to everyone—from our co-workers to our neighbors.

Evangelist Billy Graham sums it up so eloquently:

Evil is real, and sometimes force is the only way to defeat it. I am convinced, however, that military power alone is not sufficient to turn the tide of hatred and fanaticism that threatens to engulf us. Ultimately we need God's help, and only He can turn back the tide and bring lasting peace to our world. That is why we need to pray. The Bible says, "God is our refuge and strength, an ever present help in trouble. ...He makes wars cease to the ends of the earth" (Psalm 46:1,9).

Yes, we should pray for peace, and we also should ask God to give wisdom to our world's leaders. But may this be a time when you seek another kind of peace—and *that is God's peace in your heart. You see, by nature we are all at war—at war with God, because of sin. But God loves us, and Christ came to end the war and reconcile us to God. The Bible says, "He came and preached peace to you" (Ephesians 2:17).*

If you have never done so, confess your sins to God and by faith ask Christ to come into your life. Then trust the future—including your family—into His hands. No, I can't guarantee everything will go the way you wish it would. But with Christ in your heart you can face the future with confidence.

This article stayed on the web site's headlines section until the war officially ended. People needed to be assured that God was with them through these difficult times. Nobody likes war but sometimes it is necessary to resort to it, as in this case.

I felt proud of all the Hispanic soldiers that fought for our nation in this war. Most of the Spanish television stations sent reporters whose main focus was telling stories about our Hispanic soldiers. There were so many soldiers and officers whose last names were Rodriguez, Martinez, Lopez, Ramirez, Torres and Gutierrez, among the many Spanish last names found.

Of course, we have so many other Hispanic veterans who have fought in previous wars. Only they understand the impact that going to war has had in their lives. But we are all thankful that they sacrificed their lives so that the rest of us can have peace in our country.

Thank you to all who have defended our nation by going to war. Words will never be enough to show our gratitude for all you have done.

Que Dios los cuide siempre y que les de su paz!

Gracias soldados!

We Are All Americans

The media says that Hispanics are now the largest minority in America. That's terrific news for all of us that fall under this category. We are now seeing, how more than ever, American companies are trying to court us. We are no longer being ignored. Rather, we are being respected. It's a great time to be a Hispanic or Latino (whichever name it is you prefer) in this wonderful nation of ours.

We are Hispanic, but let us not forget that above all we are all Americans. Many of us have changed for the better after arriving in this country. Many others have had the honor of being born and raised in this country. We have to be thankful for the American heart, which is compassionate, giving, and caring. Those Americans, who trace their origins back to England, Germany, Ireland, Italy, Israel, Africa, and many other nations, were the ones who welcomed us into their home. Now, we consider it our home as well. Now, they consider us a part of them. How awesome, that we can all now accept one another and that there are only a few visible prejudices that keep us apart.

The new generation of Hispanics doesn't remember the days when segregation existed in this country. They don't remember those times when Hispanics were not allowed in certain restaurants, movie theaters, schools, churches, and other public places. Yes, this is a great time to be a Hispanic. A great time to be who you were meant to be. A time to not be ashamed of the color of your skin, your last name, your traditional food, your accent, your ideas, your talents, your Hispanic soul.

Above all, this is the greatest time to be an American.

I am proud to be Hispanic and Latino, but more so, I am proud to be an American.

Enjoy your life. Enjoy your moments with your loved ones. Enjoy the freedom that America offers. We couldn't have it any better.

May God Bless Us All!

0-595-29940-7